THE Tarot BIBLE

THE

Tarot

BIBLE

A handbook for the tarot practitioner

CHARTWELL BOOKS, INC.

A QUANTUM BOOK

This edition published in 2010 by
CHARTWELL BOOKS, INC
A division of BOOK SALES, INC
276 Fifth Avenue, Suite 206
New York, New York 10001
USA

ISBN-13: 978-0-7858-2725-2

ISBN-10: 0-7858-2725-0

Produced by
Quantum Publishing Ltd
The Old Brewery
6 Blundell Street
London N7 9BH

QUMTBAW

Project Editor: Samantha Warrington
Production Manager: Rohana Yusof
Publisher: Sarah Bloxham

Packaged by Quadrum Solutions

Printed in China by Midas Printing International Ltd.

Contents

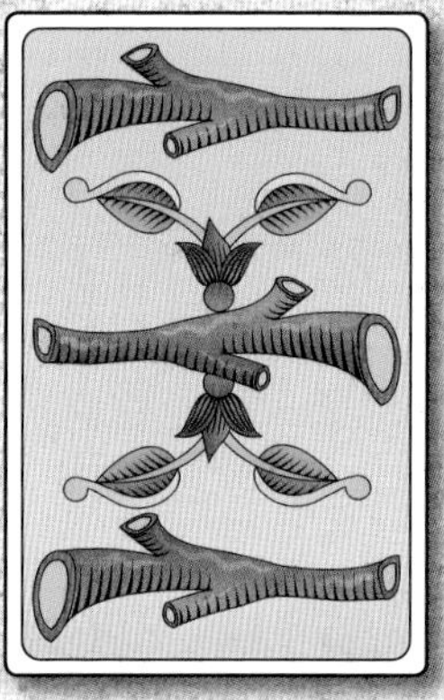

Introduction 6

The Ethics of Tarot Reading 8

The History of the Tarot 10

Conducting a Reading 16

The Bohemian Spread 18

The Romany Draw 20

The Celtic Cross 22

General Questions 24

General Answers 28

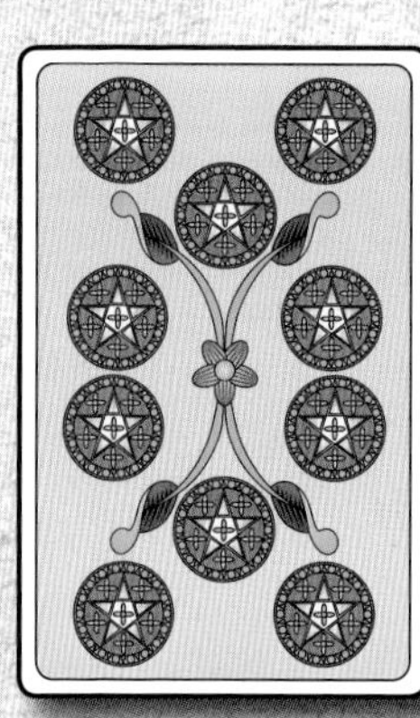

The Bohemian Spread 34

Love and Desires 36

Love and the Unexpected 46

Career and Luck 56

Career and Present Influences 66

Full Reading 76

The Romany Draw 82

Love and Romance 84

Career and Success 94

Health and Well-being 104

Personal Character 116

Full Reading 126

The Celtic Cross 130

Major Arcana: Influences 132

Major Arcana: Feelings 140

Major Arcana: Final Outcome 150

Minor Arcana: General 160

Minor Arcana: Final Outcome 170

Full Reading 182

The Tarot Deck 186

The Major Arcana 188

The Minor Arcana 200

Index 218

INTRODUCTION

Many people are able to quote the meanings of a single tarot card, but the real skill is being able to interpret several cards, taking into account the modified meanings cards can take on when seen in combination with others. This book is written for those people who already have some knowledge of the tarot but who need practice in interpreting the cards in the context of a spread.

Questions and answers

The book sets up theoretical readings using three of the more popular tarot spreads—the Bohemian Spread, the Romany Draw, and the Celtic Cross—with a chapter for each. Sample questions and card combinations are posed for you to answer. Once you have made your own interpretation, simply turn the page and compare it to my own. For each spread there is also an example of a full reading that takes all the cards that appear in the spread into account in the final interpretation. Working your way through the chapters will help you sharpen your reading ability.

Layers of meaning

All tarot cards have a primary meaning as well as several subsidiary ones. Although the primary meaning is usually the most significant, this is not always the case. It is therefore important to study the entire structure of the spread, assessing the positive or negative influence that one card may have on another, and how this could affect your final interpretation. Remember also that both the primary and subsidiary meanings of a card could be relevant; they may refer to the same matter but from different angles, or to another matter that is important to the person for whom you are giving the reading.

Each tarot card has several different meanings, all of which may effect the reading.

Personal interpretation

Learning to read the tarot is like learning a language—you need to learn all the rules before you can bend them. However, whether you are a beginner or more experienced reader, your psychic sense, like your past history, is individual and unique to you, so focusing on a particular tarot card could bring a different picture or message to mind than its traditional meaning. Perhaps, when reading my interpretations, you will see aspects that I seem to have ignored. I have given you what I think is the most vital outcome, but you may see an additional element or another choice. That is for you to decide. As your psychic sense grows, you will sense what the cards are telling you and what the interpretation should be.

Each card in a spread affects all the others, just like a drop of water falling into a calm pool creates its own impact and then sends out ever-widening ripples.

THE ETHICS OF TAROT READING

> "LET NO MAN ENTER THIS PLACE, SAVE HIS HANDS BE PURE."

In Ancient Greece, this quotation was carved over the entrance to the Temple of Apollo that guarded the cave of the Delphic Oracle. It illustrates the reverence the Ancient Greeks displayed toward the priests, priestesses, and sibyls whose advice and prophecies were believed to be messages from the gods.

The sixth sense

Telepathic and psychic abilities are often called the sixth sense. Many people believe this sense to be present in a large percentage of the population in varying degrees. However, development and guidance are required for its constructive use. Devices such as tarot cards and crystal balls are basically methods of trancing the mind, because it is when the mind's mental activity is quieted and the point of focus set that the sixth sense comes into play. The symbols of the tarot cards then act as guidelines for the messages that come through clairvoyantly. For some psychics, however, the sixth sense is so overwhelmingly strong that there is no need for such devices.

Spiritual significance

The spiritual significance of tarot cards lifts them above being mere fortune-telling devices. With their accent on evolution, spiritual growth, karmic forces, and cosmic consciousness, they are concerned less with material existence and more with the moral triumphs and failures that make up humankind's progress through life. Tarot readings involve both emotional and practical matters, reflecting the character and spiritual development of the person who is the subject of the reading. Experiences and emotions that could have resulted in his or her present situation or outlook on

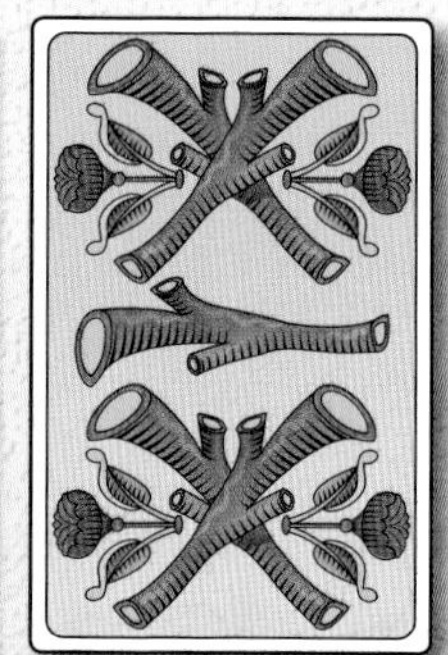

Items such as tarot cards and crystal balls are simply tools to help you to focus your mind and call your sixth sense into play.

life are revealed. Some cards also denote spiritual lessons that must be learned before future happiness can be achieved.

Positive interpretation

Tarot cards must never be approached in a spirit of levity or used for personal gain, and because of the vulnerability of the person having the reading, the cards must always be interpreted with a positive attitude, even if their meaning is mainly negative. In this way, he or she will be encouraged to listen to the positive counsel given, and by changing direction, attitudes, or actions, hopefully achieve happiness. Never dwell too much on the negative aspects of the cards or you could destroy a person's confidence. Remember that everybody can learn from their mistakes, change their attitude, and work toward a fulfilled and happy future, and by giving a positive interpretation you can help to steer them toward self-knowledge and self-fulfillment.

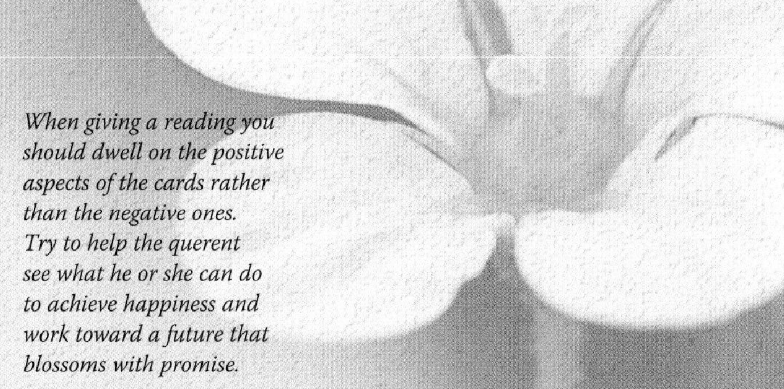

When giving a reading you should dwell on the positive aspects of the cards rather than the negative ones. Try to help the querent see what he or she can do to achieve happiness and work toward a future that blossoms with promise.

THE HISTORY OF THE TAROT

The early history of the 78 Tarot cards is shrouded in mystery and speculation. Some believe that they derived from the sacred books of ancient Egypt. Others that they originated in India or China, and were brought to Europe by gypsies. Some think that they were invented by a group of medieval cabalists. Influences as varied as the Greek mystery religions, Gnosticism, Neoplatonism, Hermetism, Catharism, ancient Arabian and Indian philosophies, and the Jewish cabala have been detected in their symbols. The Tarot has been claimed to enshrine the secrets of the universe and to hold the key to the true nature of human beings.

Early Cards

The oldest description we have of a set of Tarot cards dates from 1392, when three decks were bought for King Charles VI of France. The cards, commissioned from an artist – thought to have been Jacques Gringonneur, who was also an astrologer and cabalist — were undoubtedly magnificent, as befitted their royal beneficiary. Seventeen cards, painted on vellum, with gold edgings and depicted in silver, lapis lazuli, and a dark red pigment known as "mummy's dust," were long thought to belong to this set. They are now, however, judged to be Italian and of later manufacture.

Tarot cards almost certainly preceded playing cards designed for entertainment, to which they are related. Examples exist of 15th-century decks of cards used for games and also for education – a set depicting the order of the universe, for example. But records show that playing cards were widespread

The Tarot has been linked to medieval Italian pageants, known as Triumphs, and the earliest cards may have been gifts from the artists who worked on the pageants to their patrons. Such Triumphs may be the origin of our word "Trumps" for the major cards.

in Europe earlier than this. Gambling with cards was banned in what is now Germany as early as 1378, but in 1379 card-playing was one of the events at a festival in Brussels, and, in the same year, the ledgers of the Duke of Brabant (also in modern-day Belgium) recorded money paid for a set of cards. In the following year the Code of Nuremberg permitted card-playing, and three years later it was sanctioned in Florence. But in 1397 people in Paris were still prohibited from playing cards on working days.

The imagery of the Tarot and other cards has been linked with the pageants held in Italian cities in medieval times. Called Triumphs, these were usually commissioned by one of the noble families and were dramatic stories with a moral theme, possibly related to the ancient mystery plays. Arranged in honor of a dynastic marriage or a visiting Church dignitary, or to celebrate a saint's day, the pageants developed into costly and complicated tableaux that eventually required the invention by engineers of mechanisms to animate them, and the designs of famous artists, such as Leonardo da Vinci, to stage them. A card game named Triumphs existed from the 14th century, and may have developed from cards commemorating one such pageant, commissioned by the patron or presented to him as a souvenir by the grateful artist.

The Knights Templars

Another, more widely supported theory holds that the cards were invented by the Knights Templars, an ascetic and military order of knights formed from among the Crusaders in about 1118, under the leadership of Hugh de Payen. Their mission was to protect pilgrims and guard the routes to the Holy Land. In time, the order became so powerful and wealthy that it was perceived as a threat by King Philip IV of France. In 1307 he confiscated its property, and charged the Knights with heresy on the basis of what many now believe to have been false testimony. The Templars were accused of worshiping an idol known as Baphomet, and having statues in their meeting places which were considered by the Church to represent the devil. The figures were depictions of Mithras, a Persian god, whose worship spread to ancient Rome and was popular throughout the Roman Empire, because of its promise of human redemption and eternal life. Mithras was associated with the sun and with astrology, and his ritual involved secret initiation ceremonies in underground temples. Many of the Knights Templars, including their leader, were tortured into confessions – publicly renounced later in the case of the leader – and were burned at the stake.

The Knights Templars were officially disbanded in 1312, but groups survived, and the mystique that had surrounded the Order for 200 years continued to intrigue people down the centuries. To this day, individuals and organizations claim to be the inheritors of the Templars' secrets and their rites. The Knights did indulge in mysterious practices; symbolic carvings in their meeting places suggest that they may have engaged in alchemy, mystic geometry, numerology, and astrology (identical with astronomy at the time). By virtue of their military role in the Near East, they were exposed to unfamiliar ideas derived from Islamic and Judaic culture. They were influenced also by their Cathar recruits, who espoused the beliefs of Gnosticism – a system that combined mythology, ancient Greek philosophy, ancient religions,

Crusaders such as the Knights Templars (right) were renowned for their secret rituals. Their symbology can be found in many Tarot decks.

and Christianity, that viewed matter as evil and emphasized a personal union with the divine. Whether the Templars worshiped idols, or merely adorned their meeting places with emblems considered appropriate for a military order, we do not know. However, symbols linked to them can be found in many Tarot decks, and the picture of the Devil in 18th-century decks – perhaps inspired by a contemporary revival of interest in the order – is consistent with the Mithraic statues associated with the Templars.

The Wisdom of Ancient Egypt

The view of the Tarot as a compendium of ancient mystical wisdom was adopted with particular enthusiasm in 18th-century France. This was the "Age of Enlightenment," prior to the French Revolution, when humanitarian ideals were burgeoning and dogma was once again being challenged. Secret and semi-secret societies were founded, which looked to the Templars as earlier exemplars of the anti-clerical ideas that were in the air. Freemasons of the day claimed for themselves the inheritance of the Templars' rituals and their arcane secrets.

In 1773 the French scholar and freemason Antoine Court de Gebelin wrote a series of books entitled Le Monde Primitif, which discussed the customs, science, and religion of the ancient world and compared them with the civilization of his day. In volume 8, he examined the Tarot and pronounced it to be of ancient Egyptian origin. He asserted that the Tarot was a remnant of the sacred book of the Egyptian god Thoth, patron of scribes and magicians, whose functions included weighing the human heart during the judgment after death. The Greeks and Romans associated Thoth with their messenger god Hermes/Mercury. They regarded him as the founder of alchemy, in which Mercury, the element named for the god, is accorded great power. Thoth

Egyptian artifacts brought to Europe by Napoleon in the 18th century excited the popular imagination, and the Tarot was widely believed to have originated in ancient Egypt.

acquired the title Hermes Trismegistus (the Thrice-Great Hermes) from the Neoplatonists, who named alchemy "the hermetic art" in his honor. According to legend, 42 hermetic books were written at the dictation of Hermes Trismegistus, setting out the philosophy of ancient Egypt. It was de Gebelin's belief that the surviving fragments, in the form of the Tarot, had been preserved by the Gypsies following their exodus from ancient Egypt.

When he first encountered the Tarot, de Gebelin realized that the cards were of considerable antiquity, and he noted that although they had been used for centuries in Belgium, Italy, Germany, and Spain, for gambling and for divination, they were little known in France outside the south of the country and the port of Marseilles in particular. This was an area inhabited by large numbers of Gypsies. The Gypsies, who reached France in the 15th century, were initially thought to have come from Egypt (the name Gypsy derives from "Egyptian"), although they originated from India, and migrated through Persia to Europe.

De Gebelin's ideas were enthusiastically taken up by a Parisian barber named Alliette, who rose to fame as a fortune-teller under the pseudonym Etteilla (his name spelled backward). His book on the Tarot, published in 1775, and a deck of his own devising, were notable more on account of his showmanship and financial flair than for the authenticity of his research. He stressed the divinatory aspect of the cards, and their links with astrology and the cabala, but his alterations and interpretations were denigrated by scholars and subsequently disregarded. Etteilla was not the only French fortune-teller to turn to print. One of his most famous successors was Marie Le Normand, whose reputation was assured when she predicted Napoleon's marriage to Josephine. She developed her own methods, and her book on cartomancy and her own set of cards, based loosely on the Tarot, are still available.

Toward the end of the 18th century, de Gebelin's theory gained impetus from the interest surrounding Napoleon's expedition to Egypt. The arrival in France of tablets, statues, papyri, and other antiquities, bearing their mysterious hieroglyphics, prompted a fascination with everything Egyptian. Excitement was succeeded by disappointment for some, however, when the Rosetta stone, discovered in 1799, which provided the key to ancient Egyptian writing, failed to reveal any links with the Tarot.

Early 19th-century scholars, such as Jean Duchesne (writing in 1844) and William Chatto (writing in 1848), dismissed the Egyptian theory as too far-fetched, and declared the Tarot to be European, and Samuel Singer, writing in 1816, had preferred the 15th-century finding of Covelluzo, that the cards had originated in Arabia.

A New Deck

In 1916, the American occultist and writer Arthur Edward Waite, also a Golden Dawn member, worked with artist Pamela Colman Smith on the design of a new Tarot deck. Known as the Rider-Waite deck – Rider comes from the name of its London publisher – it departed from tradition by incorporating Rosicrucian concepts into a number of the major arcana and, more strikingly, recreating the minor arcana to show scenes instead of a pattern of symbols. Although Waite and Smith received much criticism from occultists and scholars for their amendments to age-old principles, and for the unattractiveness of the new deck, their interpretations made the Tarot much more accessible to those who found other decks difficult to understand, and the Rider deck is one of the most widely used today.

Enduring Power

Explanations of the history and meaning of the Tarot continue to be suggested. Whatever its origins, however, there was almost certainly never a single way of interpreting the cards. So evocative is their symbolism that no two people are likely to draw exactly the same associations from them. The mystery of the Tarot may lie beyond words, and the wisdom we can draw from it may be only as much as we need to aid our own perceptions. There is no doubt, however, that the cards embody an aura of mystery and a power that should never be misused.

Conducting a Reading

The person conducting the reading is referred to as the reader; the person having the reading is known as the querent. Start by asking the querent if he or she has a specific question in mind—this could be about love or career, for example—or whether a general reading taking all aspects of life into account would be preferred.

Choosing a significator

Some readers start by choosing a card to represent the querent. This card is known as the significator, so-called because it signifies inner feelings and outer events surrounding the querent. It is left face up on the table throughout the reading. Most readers use the court cards of the Minor Arcana for this purpose. Kings represent men over 35; queens symbolize women over 21; knights denote men between 21 and 35; and knaves signify both male and female youths under 21. The suit you choose will depend on the querent's coloring; older people with gray or whitehair are usually represented by Pentacles or Cups.

Pentacles: red, light blond, or gray hair; fair or freckled skin; blue or gray eyes

Cups: blond, light brown, or gray hair; fair to medium skin; blue or gray eyes

Wands: light or dark brown hair; light olive skin; brown, green, or hazel eyes

Swords: dark brown or black hair; dark skin; dark brown or black eyes

Choose the knave, knight, queen, or king to represent the querent, depending on his or her age and gender.

Small spreads are used by readers when answering a specific question or examining one particular aspect of the querent's life.

Selecting the spread

There are hundreds of different tarot spreads, so the one you choose will largely be a case of personal preference. As a guideline, many readers prefer to use small spreads when answering a specific question or examining one particular aspect of the querent's life, and more complex spreads for general readings and overviews. The instructions for three popular spreads are given on the following pages.

Relaxation and Empathy

To begin a reading it is important to relax the mind, so that it is open to the messages the Tarot symbols will send you. Once you have chosen which spread to use, spend a few moments meditating or praying for guidance. You can also protect yourself by visualizing a shining gold ring encircling your body and then closing up around your chest. Remember that in every reading, no matter what negative messages the cards bring, you must always try to put yourself in the querent's place and interpret them in the kindest way possible.

The particular suit you choose for the significator will depend on the coloring of the querent.

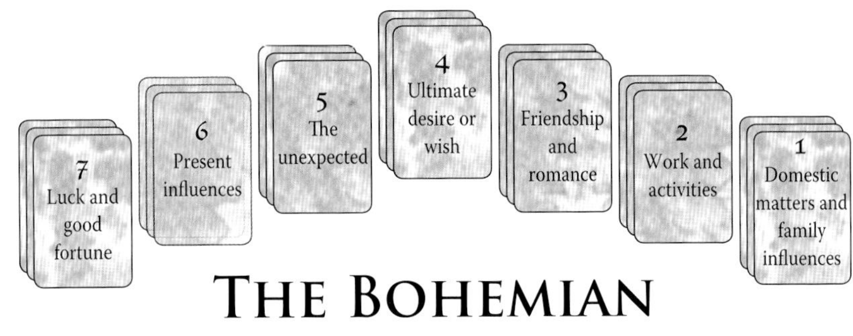

THE BOHEMIAN SPREAD

The Bohemian Spread is used to give an overview of the querent's life and situation. Each card is influenced slightly by the card beside it, and this must be taken into account when assessing the whole spread.

Choosing the cards

Start by shuffling the deck, then put it face down on the table. Ask the querent to cut the deck into three piles with the left hand. Turn the piles over and memorize the top card from each, which can often relate to the outcome of the reading. Put the three piles of cards back together and spread them out on the table in the shape of a fan. Ask the querent to choose 21 cards from anywhere in the deck. Make sure the cards are kept in the order they are chosen. Place the first seven cards face up on the table in a triangular shape, working from left to right. Repeat with the next seven cards, placing them on top of the first seven. Repeat once again until you have seven piles of three cards.

Study the three cards in each position and assess how they affect each other before looking at the spread as a whole.

Each position on the spread relates to different aspects of life.

Evaluating the cards

Each position on the spread relates to different aspects of life. Start with the cards in position four, then look at positions five, six, and seven before returning to the beginning and assessing positions one, two and three. Evaluate the three cards in each position both in terms of how they affects each other and their location in the spread. Finally, study the spread as a whole, looking at how the cards in each position affect the cards in the other positions. If the meaning of the spread is unclear, consider the three cards you saw when the querent cut the deck and allow these to influence your interpretations.

Make sure the cards are kept in the order they are chosen.

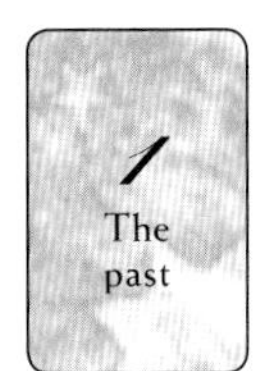

THE ROMANY DRAW

The Romany Draw is used to answer a specific question. Many tarot readers use it after having done a larger, more detailed spread that looks at the querent's life as a whole but has failed to address a particular concern of the querent.

Choosing the cards

Shuffle the cards, place them face down on the table, and ask the querent to use his or her left hand to cut them into three piles. Turn the piles over and memorize the top card from each. You may find that these three cards clarify the outcome of the reading. Put the cards back together again and fan them out on the table in front of the querent. Ask the querent to choose three cards, one at a time, from anywhere in the deck and place them face up on the table from left to right.

After the querent has chosen the three cards for the spread, leave the remaining cards fanned out on the table in case you need to repeat the process to clarify the reading.

Study the cards from left to right and evaluate their meanings in relation to their location in the spread and the question being asked.

Evaluating the cards

The card on the left denotes the past, the card in the center relates to the present, and the card on the right indicates the future. Study the cards from left to right and evaluate their meanings in relation to their location in the spread and the question being asked. If the answer to the question is unclear, consider the three cards you saw when the querent cut the deck and assess how these might affect the outcome. If there is still no definite conclusion, ask the querent to choose three more cards from those fanned out on the table, then another three. You will now have nine cards to assess, three each for the past, present, and future. These cards, plus the three you initially saw, should give the solution.

The card on the left denotes the past, the card in the center relates to the present, and the card on the right indicates the future.

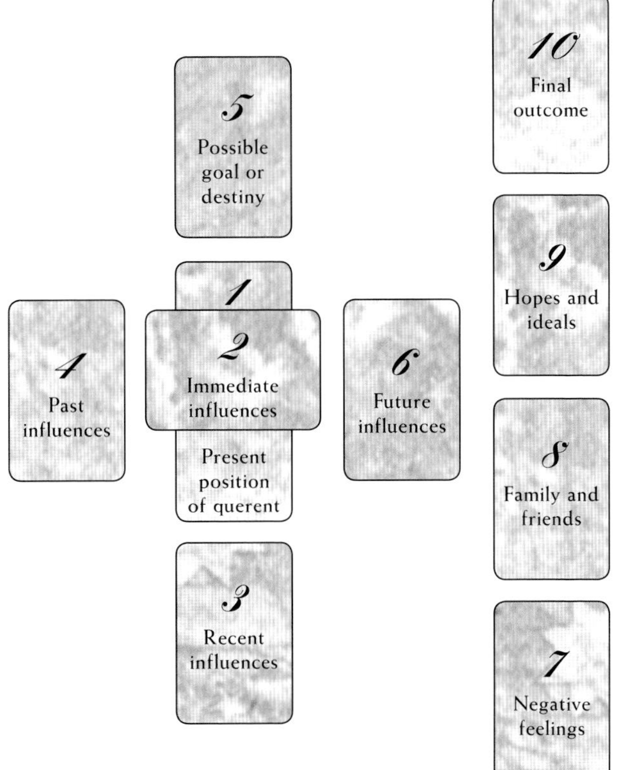

THE CELTIC CROSS

The Celtic Cross gives an overall view of the querent's life and foretells future prospects. Some tarot readers use only the spiritually strong Major Arcana, while others prefer to use the whole deck since this gives a more balanced view of daily life. If the final outcome is unclear or the cards appear contradictory, the reader may then repeat the spread using only the Major Arcana.

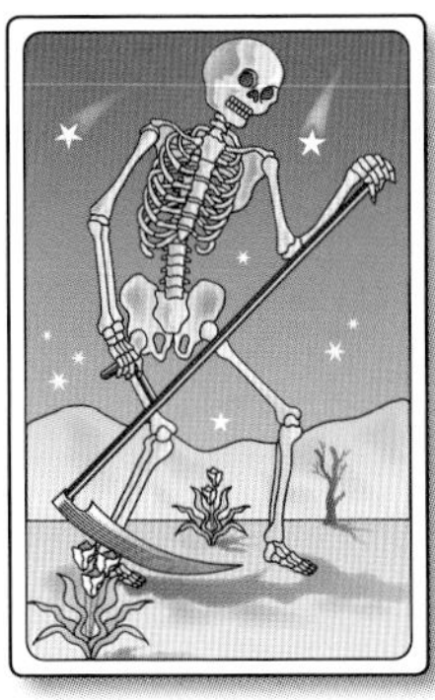

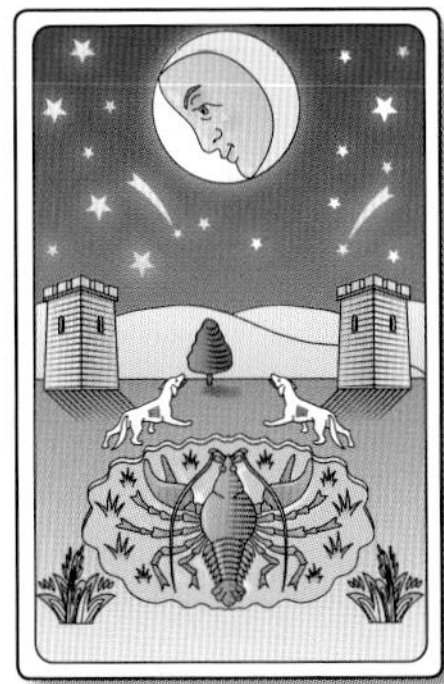

Choosing the cards

Shuffle the deck and ask the querent to cut it into three piles with the left hand. Memorize the top card from each pile; these sometimes indicate the outcome of the spread. Put the three piles of cards back together and fan them out on the table. Ask the querent to choose ten cards at random, making sure the cards are kept in the order they are chosen. Lay out the cards in the positions of the Celtic Cross.

Evaluating the cards

Start by studying the tenth card, denoting the final outcome, then check the card in the fifth position because these two cards sometimes cancel each other out. Next, look at all the remaining positions, paying particular attention to strongly positive or negative cards. Finally, consider all the cards together and formulate your overall interpretation, bearing in mind that the card in position ten can sometimes enhance, change, or negate the result expected from the cards in the earlier positions. If the cards are unclear, take into account the three cards you saw when the querent cut the deck.

If the meaning of the spread is unclear, consider how the three cards you saw when the querent cut the deck may clarify the reading.

GENERAL QUESTIONS

These questions look at the general aspects of conducting a reading, from choosing your tarot cards and the particular spread you use to interpreting reversed cards and dealing with skeptical querents. Refer to pages 28-33 for the answers to these questions.

Q1 There are lots of tarot decks to choose from. Which is the best deck to use and should you use the same deck all the time or can you use several different ones?

Q2 What is the best way to look after your tarot cards when they are not in use and should you allow anyone else to touch them?

Q3 How do you create an appropriate atmosphere and get into the right mind-set for a tarot reading?

Q4 Is it possible to read tarot cards even if you are not psychic, and can you use the cards to help develop your psychic powers?

Q5 What should you do if more than one person comes for a reading, such as a group of friends or a married couple?

Q6 Should the querent ask a specific question when having a reading or is it better if he or she says nothing at all?

Q7 Is it alright to make up your own tarot spreads or should you only use well-known ones such as the Bohemian Spread, the Romany Draw, and the Celtic Cross?

Q8 Lots of tarot books talk about reversed (upside down) cards. What significance do these have and do you have to take them into account when conducting a tarot reading?

Q9 When tarot readers say that a card is "positively aspected" or "negatively aspected," what does it mean? Also, if the cards in the spread are primarily negative, what should you tell the querent?

Q10 What should you do if the meaning of the spread is unclear, or if it does not answer a specific question posed by the querent?

Q11 There are so many cards and possible combinations, are there any tricks you can use to remember them all, and is it acceptable to refer to a book while conducting a reading?

Q12 What should you do if the querent says your interpretation doesn't make sense or comes back at a later date and says your prediction hasn't happened?

GENERAL ANSWERS

These general answers deal with questions often asked by readers. These answers deal with aspects like how to choose the tarot deck, how to store the tarot cards and many other questions. Refer to pages 24-27 for the questions to these answers.

A1 The choice of tarot cards is a matter of personal preference—most people simply choose the one they like the look of. The important thing to remember is that tarot cards are just a device that you can use to stimulate your psychic and intuitive powers, so if you feel drawn to a particular deck, then that is probably the right one for you to use. Many people use the Rider-Waite tarot deck because the main meaning of each card is illustrated pictorially, including the Minor Arcana, and this can make it easier to remember the meanings of the cards. However, the crucial factor is that you feel an intuitive connection with the cards you choose. Most people settle on a couple of different decks that they like to work with, although inexperienced readers may find it easier to use just one deck until they have learned all the meanings and gained more experience in reading them.

A2 When not in use, it is traditional to wrap tarot cards in a piece of black silk and store them in a box or velvet bag. Whether you choose to follow this tradition is up to you; it is not essential. The important thing, however, is that you treat your cards with seriousness and respect—they are not playing cards. Most tarot readers do not allow anyone else to touch their cards because they feel that the subtle energies radiating from other people could interfere with their own psychic connection with the cards. The only exception is during a reading, and even then, the querent only touches the cards once at the beginning of the reading to cut them into three piles.

A3 Flowers and low lighting can help to create a peaceful atmosphere. You may also feel more relaxed if you wear a white or blue garment. It is always best to sit alone before the querent's arrival, listening to music that calms the spirit. This will help you open up to the spiritual force that guides and protects you and the querent. Some psychics say a prayer before a reading, some meditate, and others prefer to hold the querent's hands and ask the divine spirit to give them guidance. You can also protect yourself by visualizing a shining gold ring encircling your body and then closing up around your chest. Some psychics do this to safeguard themselves against an encounter with people of a strongly combative or negative nature that can drain their energy. If you sense a loving positiveness in your querent, however, visualize building a bridge between that person and yourself.

A4 The psychic sense plays an important role in reading tarot cards, since the cards are in fact simply a stimulus to the intuitive powers and an aid to divinination. It has been estimated that 6 out of 10 people are strongly psychic and the others can develop their psychic sense if they really want to. Some people simply do not recognize they have it; others deny its existence, afraid of something they cannot explain logically; and some people even consider it satanic. One way of developing your psychic sense is to spend a few minutes each day meditating on your tarot cards and their meanings. Meditation helps to still your conscious mind and stimulate your intuitive powers. As your psychic

You can try to develop your psychic sense by meditating on your tarot cards. A good meditation trick is to focus on the flame of a candle first to help clear your mind.

ability grows, so will your sense of spiritual protection. An awareness of the spiritual dimension of life, plus a trust in the intuitional faculty, can lead to the development of a psychic sense in most people, and this sense will be peculiarly the property of each reader. This is why different tarot readers will often interpret a spread of cards in slightly—or sometimes dramatically—different ways.

A5 Give separate readings for friends, but if you are performing a reading for a couple in a long-term relationship, ask one partner to shuffle a second pack of cards while the other's cards are being read. Even if you are giving a reading for a married woman on her own, for example, you will find that her cards will also refer to events in her husband's life.

A6 Some readers prefer the querent to ask a specific question. Although this makes reading the cards easier in some ways, difficulties can arise when the answer to the question does not appear in the spread. If this happens, you will probably find that the cards are concerned with other, more important, matters. Some people who visit a tarot reader are skeptical and prefer not to ask a question so that they reveal nothing of themselves, leaving the reader to foretell their future with the information given. To gain the querent's confidence, it can be a good idea to give a first reading without anything specific being asked. Then perform a second reading if the querent wants to ask a question, although it is likely that the first reading will already have answered it.

You may find that putting some fresh flowers on the table where you intend to conduct a reading will help to create a relaxed and positive ambience.

A7 Readers have been developing their own spreads since tarot cards were first used for divination. Many different spreads can be found in numerous publications. If you are new to tarot reading, it is best to use one of the traditional spreads—after all, if a spread has endured over a long period of time, it is likely to be effective for most readers. However, once you become familiar with all 78 tarot cards and most of their meanings (there are so many it is unusual to find someone who can remember them all without sometimes referring to a book), and have proved your psychic ability with successful readings, you may design your own spread, provided you address every important aspect of life.

A8 Reversals were only introduced in the mid-19th century, possibly by Etteilla, the French barber-turned-clairvoyant. Some readers regard reversed cards as having the opposite of their usual meaning, so negative cards become more positive and vice versa. However, many tarot readers prefer to ignore reversals, believing that they make things more difficult than they need to be. Most cards have meanings that denote both positive and negative aspects of life—very few are either wholly positive or negative—and these are sufficient to give a full and detailed reading. So although some authorities do believe in reversals, the most important approach is to listen to your inner voice and develop your psychic ability. However, whether you choose to use reversals or not, the meanings of all tarot cards can be altered, enhanced, or diminished by the cards around them—that is, all cards may be positively or negatively aspected by having positive or negative cards nearby.

A9 The term "aspected" refers to the configuration of the cards in relation to one another. When one card is said to be positively aspected, well-aspected, or favorably aspected, it means that another card with a primarily positive meaning is next to or near it. Similarly, the terms negatively aspected and badly aspected indicate that a primarily negative card is nearby. When several positive cards appear together in a spread, they will obviously affect your interpretation favorably, while negative cards will produce a less positive result. When a positive and negative card are next to each other, they temper each other's meanings. However, even the most negative cards have some positive meanings, and you should emphasize these in your interpretation—readings should be constructive, not destructive.

A10 Many tarot readers start by laying out a second spread to see if the cards become clearer. When using the Romany Draw, for example, it is not uncommon for a reader to have to lay out nine cards instead of the usual three in order to make an interpretation. If the cards are still unclear, it is sometimes a good idea to try using a different spread. Another good solution is to use two packs of tarot cards. Give one to the querent to hold, getting him or her to shuffle the deck and split it into three piles. Meanwhile, you should perform a reading with the other pack. Compare the top card in each of the three piles in the querent's pack with those in the spread that you have laid out. Although the two sets of cards may differ in minor matters, usually they repeat each other, which will help you check that you have interpreted the cards correctly. This is also useful if you have a particularly strong-minded querent, because you may find yourself telling him or her what he or she wants to hear, not what is actually going to happen.

A11 It usually takes years of practice to remember all the meanings of the tarot, and even the most experienced readers sometimes have to check the meaning of a particular card now and again. However, although it is acceptable to refer to a book, it can be distracting and may break your focus on the querent, so memorizing the meanings of the cards is always preferable. You could start by writing all the meanings of each card onto a label and paste it on the back of the card. You could study one card every night, building a story around it and concentrating on the imagery before you go to sleep. The next day, try to see aspects of the card in the people you meet and the events that take place. This will help to reinforce the abstract meanings of the cards by relating them to real occurrences. When you do become more familiar with all the cards and their meanings, you will find in time that you will form your own interpretation of each card and card combination based on your own intuition. Later, this will be enlarged by your own psychic experience. Most tarot readers find that their relationship with the cards evolves over time.

Most tarot cards have both positive and negative meanings. For example, a card could indicate that the querent is about to face a difficult task or hardship but will be richly rewarded when it is over.

A12 Some predictions occur almost immediately, while others take a long time to be proven correct—it can even take several years. If your prediction makes no sense, and you have taken all the subsidiary meanings of each card into account, offer the querent another reading at another time, but do not be surprised if you get the same result. If you get a different result, it could be that there was something happening in your own life that was transmitted to the cards. Similarly, a querent with a strong personality could have transmitted his or her wishes to you, and you have interpreted those rather than the cards in the spread, giving the result the querent wanted instead of the one that was really in the cards. Another possibility is that the querent is reluctant to accept his or her fate and can be strong enough to delay its occurrence. If this is the case, it will simply be a matter of time before your interpretation is proven correct.

The Bohemian Spread

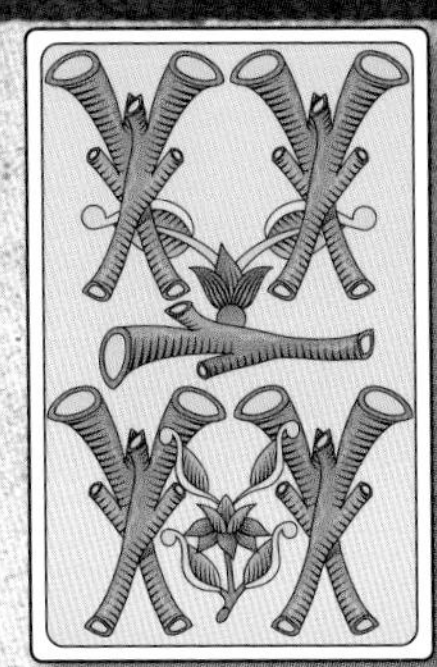

This chapter examines combinations of cards in the Bohemian Spread, which is used to give a general overview of the querent's life. The questions are organized into four themes—love and desires; love and the unexpected; career and luck; and career and present influences. The spread has seven positions, with three cards in each position. An example of a full reading that looks at all 21 cards is given at the end of the chapter.

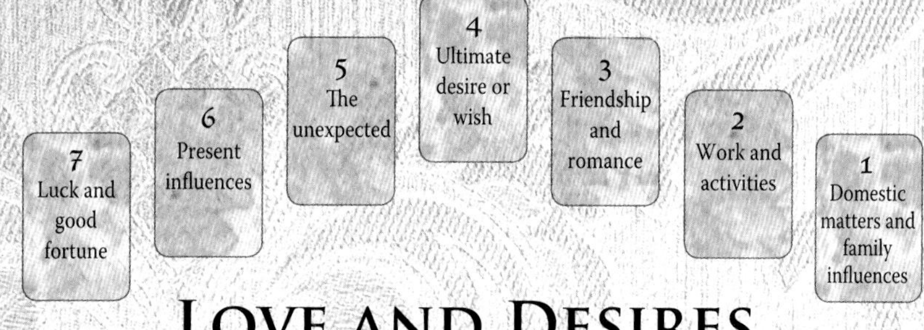

LOVE AND DESIRES QUESTIONS

These questions look at the cards in position three, friendship and romance, and then examine how the cards in position four, ultimate desire or wish, affect them. Refer to page 18-19 for instructions on how to do the Bohemian Spread; see pages 40-45 for the answers to these questions.

Q1 What do the Six of Cups, the Queen of Wands, and the Sun in position three indicate will happen in the querent's love life?

Q2 How do the Four of Wands, the Empress, and the Knave of Cups in position four affect the meaning of the cards in Question 1?

Q3 Do the Three of Swords, the Hanged Man, and the Two of Cups in position three symbolize a positive or negative romantic outlook for the querent?

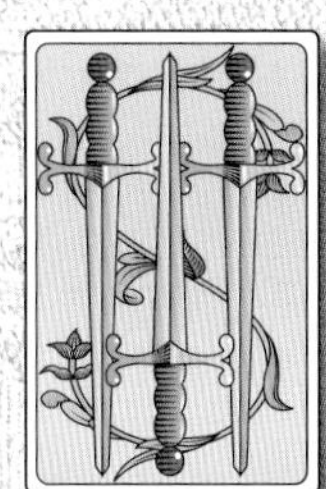

Q4 What do the Ace of Cups, the Six of Swords, and the Five of Wands in position four signify, and how should they be interpreted in relation to the cards in Question 3?

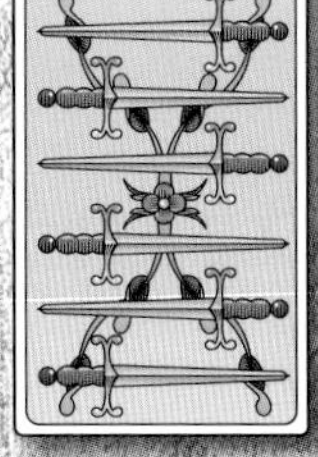
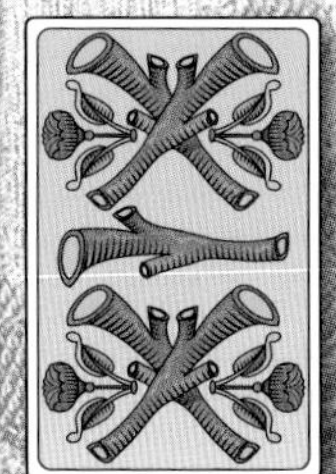

Q5 In position three, do the Knight of Cups, the Knight of Pentacles, and the Two of Cups denote happiness in romance?

Q6 How should the Three of Cups, the Lovers, and the Nine of Cups in position four be interpreted in relation to the combination of cards in Question 5?

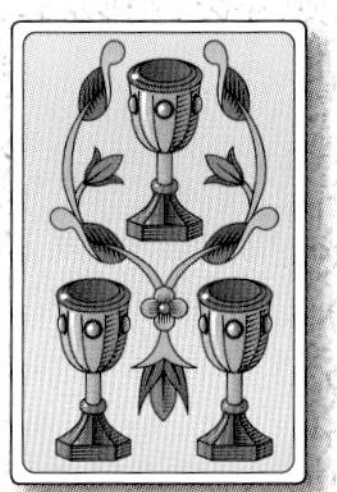

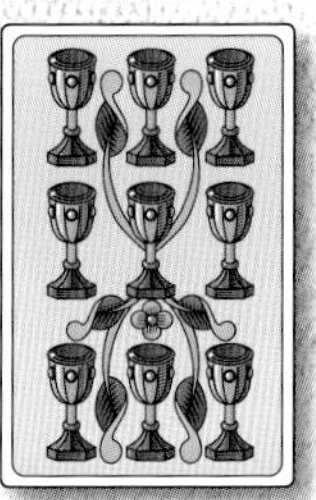

Q7 In position three, what do the Three of Swords, the Moon, and the Lovers signify in the areas of friendship and romance?

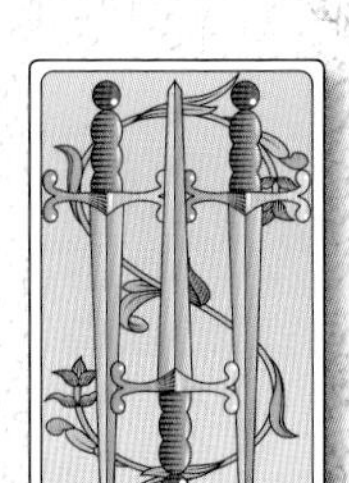

Q8 How would you evaluate the effect of the Queen of Wands, the Hermit, and the Nine of Wands in position four on the cards described in Question 7?

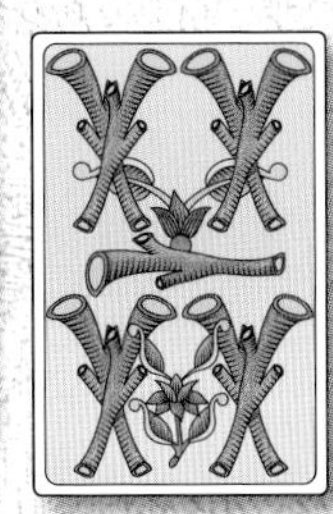

Q9 What meaning would you give to the Three of Swords, Justice, and the Hanged Man in position three?

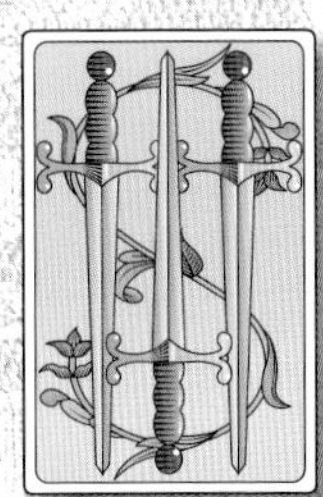

Q10 Bearing the cards in Question 9 in mind, how would you interpret the Three of Pentacles, the Chariot, and the World in position four?

7 6 5 4 3 2 1

Love and Desires Answers

A1 The Six of Cups signifies that past contacts or work will influence the present, bringing benefits either in the shape of a major ambition, the return of an old friend, or a new romance with its roots in the past. The Queen of Wands represents a tolerant, intuitive, strong, generous, protective, and confident woman who can be artistically creative. She is a good friend but a bad enemy if negatively aspected. However, here the Queen of Wands is followed by the Sun, one of the most positive cards in the deck. The Sun symbolizes achievement against all odds, realizing an ambition, studies completed, health, energy, material comfort, and the end of self-deception. The main meanings that relate to position three, friendship and romance, are harmony in relationships and the gift of gratitude. So this combination indicates that the querent will have a love affair with someone who has a connection with the past and will have great happiness. The Queen of Wands can be either the querent if female, the new lover, or someone who will be instrumental in bringing them together.

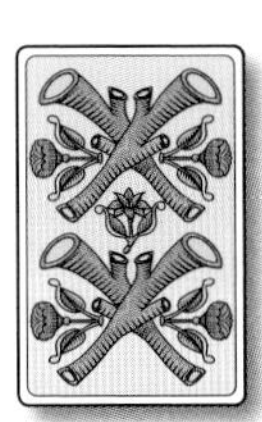

A2 The Four of Wands represents a successful designer or inventor, combining beauty and ideas to create perfect work. It can also indicate a rest from work, a peaceful vacation, gathering the harvest after a long period of toil, close family ties, harmonious relationships, and romance. The Empress signifies artistic inspiration, creative ability, intuitive emotion, the positive aspects of home, hearth, and motherhood, harmonious growth, physical and creative energy, love, protection, material wealth, femininity, fertility, and a happy marriage. The Knave of Cups is a person under 21, loyal, meditative, and artistic, who can be overly imaginative, overly emotional, and self-deceptive. It also indicates news, a message, new business methods, and what is relevant here, a change that transforms the future and the birth of a baby. When in position four, ultimate desire or wish, these cards indicate that the querent's desires are for lifelong happiness and a child, which complements the meaning of the cards in Answer 1.

A3 The Three of Swords represents an upheaval, disruption, or separation. This could be permanent or temporary, depending on the surrounding cards. It also indicates pain followed by healing and a sense that the ground has been cleared for a better future. The Hanged Man, a deeply spiritual card, means inner strength, intuition, occult power, hardship, loss, a sacrifice that transforms and changes a life, a wise decision, and forgiveness that results in spiritual peace. The Two of Cups, a happy, positive card, signifies a lovely surprise, signing a contract or agreement, limited financial support, rivalry ended, and a partnership. It indicates that emotion and spirituality will create understanding of a partner and a permanent bond, a love affair or an engagement, a lasting friendship, and most relevantly here, a reconciliation after a parting. So in position three, friendship and romance, these cards indicate that, after a painful break-up of a relationship or marriage, the querent's emotional and spiritual capacity brings forgiveness, reconciliation, and happiness.

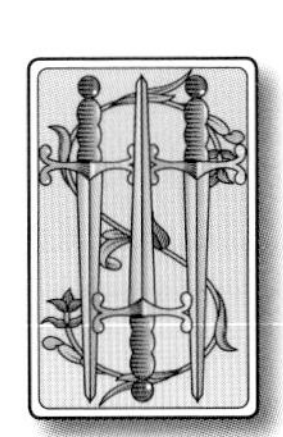

A4 The Ace of Cups symbolizes spiritual nourishment, joy in artistic work, good news, happy company, a new love affair, and if near other love cards, marriage. The Six of Swords, another positive card, means change of work, flight or travel to a better environment, success after anxiety, or obstacles removed after a period of stress. It also indicates good news brought by someone from overseas. The Five of Wands, although warning that mental ability is needed to triumph before a change for the better occurs, indicates that a determined struggle overcomes material adversity and denotes here the triumph of love over obstacles. These cards in position four, ultimate desire or wish, show that the querent, who has worked hard to achieve success, will risk traveling to a new environment or country to start fresh, and will be happy and fall in love.

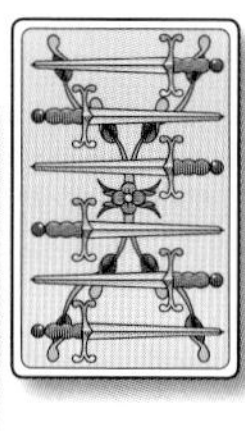
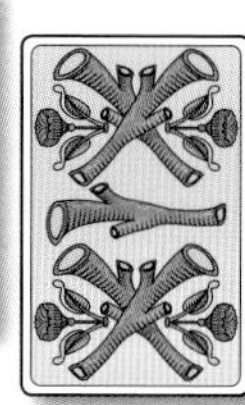

A5 The Knight of Cups represents a man under 35, highly principled, except in emotional matters, romantic, intelligent, sometimes devious, and usually egotistical. He could be a rival, friend, or lover, and signify a fated relationship that teaches a lesson. The card can also represent the bearer of a message or invitation, a proposition, or a pleasant visit. The Knight of Pentacles is a man under 35, traditional, honorable, determined,

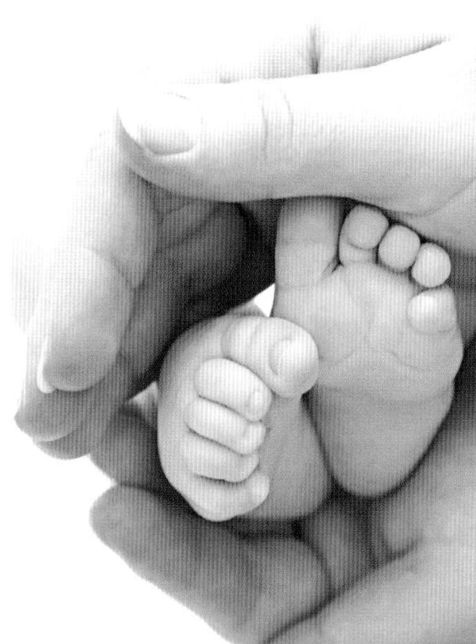

The Empress in position four, ultimate desire or wish, signifies fertility and the joys of motherhood. It indicates that the querent may want to have a child to nurture and care for.

and a lover of animals and nature. The card can also denote patience needed to finish difficult but boring work, but the relevant meanings here are those of a new acquaintance, an indiscreet flirtation, and the beginning and end of a matter. The Two of Cups means partnership, friendship, a love affair, or an engagement, and a deep understanding of another. With the Two of Cups coming after two court cards in position three, friendship and romance, they signify that indiscreet behavior will teach a lesson. So the querent must be warned that an unwise action could end a relationship, but luckily one of the lovers is spiritually mature, so there will be true forgiveness and a reconciliation.

A6 The Three of Cups represents the feminine element in nature that brings love, emotional growth, and fulfillment to a marriage or love relationship. It also means a victorious conclusion, creative ability earning fine rewards, and that the querent's sensitivity to others' needs has resulted in a generous person who receives love and friendship from others. The Lovers denotes a moment of choice, such as judging future actions in the light of good or evil, a difficult choice between physical attraction and idealistic love, or a moral choice between love and career as well as friendship, affection, harmony, and making an intuitive decision. The Nine of Cups, the wish card of the Minor Arcana, symbolizes material and emotional security, the complete fulfillment of a major wish or desire, and also good luck, good health, kindness, generosity, and intuitive awareness. However, it warns that overindulgence in life's pleasures could undermine artistic endeavors or future commitments. So the querent should be told that because of the right decision based on intuition, love, sensitivity, and generosity, the future brings all kinds of happiness, and when in position four, ultimate wish or desire, they could indicate a happy marriage or union. As a result, the cards in this position complement those in Answer 5 perfectly.

A7 These negative cards in position three, friendship and romance, reveal that there will be sorrow, heartbreak, and an emotional crisis. The Three of Swords means a separation, the severing of a partnership, a marital break-up, either temporary or permanent, a disruption or upheaval, and pain followed by healing, but it also carries the sense that the ground is clearing for something better. The Moon can mean mystery or deception resulting in an emotional crisis, and the Lovers can signify the choice between idealistic love and physical attraction. So it is no surprise to learn that the Lovers following the Moon means the illusion of love, or a false lover. What is pertinent here is that deception and lies destroy a relationship, but there is also the positive aspect that the ground is clearing for something better in the future.

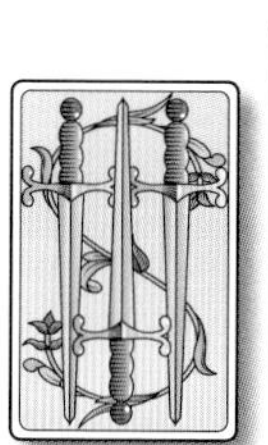

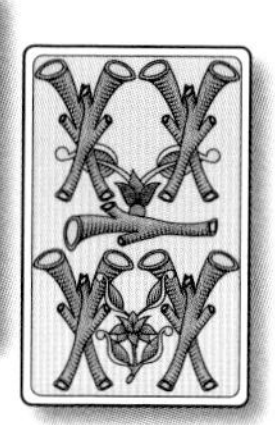

A8 The Queen of Wands could represent the querent if female, or a good friend who gives advice, is intuitive, protective, tolerant, generous, strong-willed, independant, and often artistic or creative. This card also symbolizes a successful new venture, either creative or professional. The Hermit indicates that wise advice will bring sudden insight into a problem after a journey or visit. The Nine of Wands also denotes sound advice. In addition, it signifies a lasting triumph through inner strength and integrity, a final challenge, and an expansion or success in artistic or professional fields. Since these cards are in position four, ultimate desire or wish, it is easy to see that, once the querent has overcome the problems indicated in Answer 7, he or she will accept good advice and achieve his or her desires by becoming secure professionally and happy in love. This could involve traveling to another country.

A9 In position three, friendship and romance, the Three of Swords is not a happy card because it means disruption, upheaval, either a temporary or permanent separation, a marital break-up, or a partnership broken. However, healing follows the pain, bringing a sense that something better lies in the future. If badly aspected, as it is here, it can also mean dwelling on old hurts. Justice is actually a positive card, meaning a balance of mind and personality as well as honesty and integrity, and the Hanged Man is truly spiritual, carrying connotations of sacrifice and forgiveness. However, the Hanged Man coming after Justice signifies that tolerance is needed to soften a judgment. It is therefore safe to say that, despite the querent's professional ambitions bringing prestige and wealth, a close relationship will be broken and a future reconciliation could be in doubt because tolerance and understanding of other people's failings is lacking and there will be little forgiveness for past hurts.

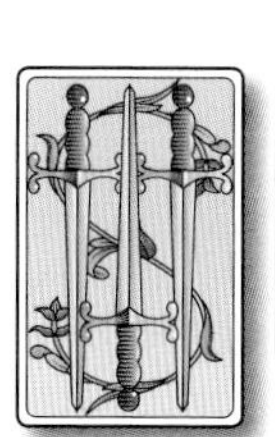

A10 These cards in position four, ultimate desire or wish, almost echo one another in their meanings and reveal that the querent has worked hard to perfect a talent or skill. This has involved triumphing over problems. There will be financial benefits and help from others. They may also signify an opportunity to expand a new business or to travel to another country. The cards are so weighted toward career that they could mean that the querent will choose to concentrate on that aspect of life instead of reconciling the problems outlined in Answer 9.

The World in position four shows that the querent is concentrating all his or her time and energy on career success and desires material wealth rather than love.

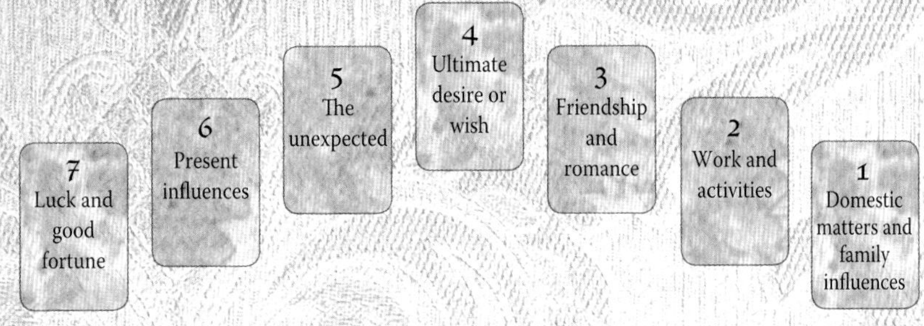

LOVE AND THE UNEXPECTED QUESTIONS

These questions look at the cards in position three, friendship and romance, and then examine how the cards in position five, the unexpected, affect them. Refer to page 18-19 for instructions on how to do the Bohemian Spread; see pages 50-55 for the answers to these questions.

Q1 How would you interpret the Eight of Swords, the Star, and the Seven of Pentacles in position three?

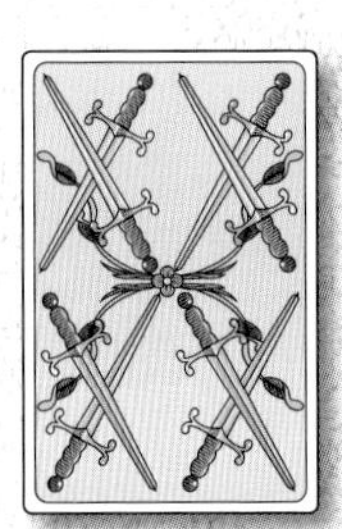

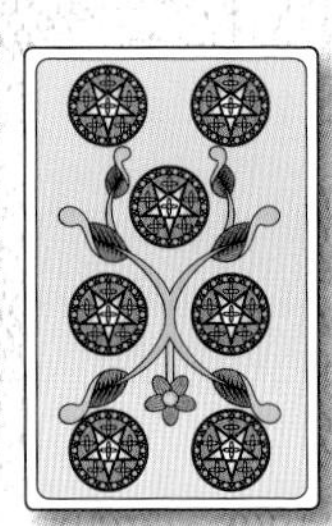

Q2 Bearing in mind your interpretation of the cards in Question 1, explain how the Chariot, the Tower, and the Ace of Cups in position five would affect the reading?

Q3 What do the Ace of Swords, the Queen of Cups, and the Four of Cups in position three indicate might happen in the querent's love life?

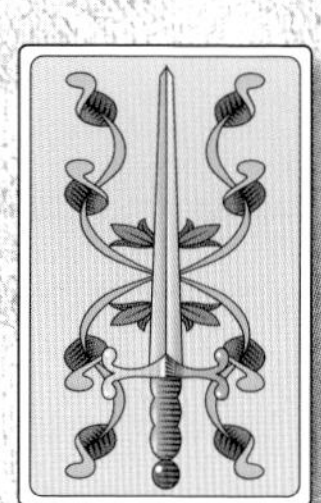

Q4 Would you assess the Moon, Justice, and the Two of Cups in position five as a positive or negative influence on the cards in Question 3?

Q5 In position three, what do the Queen of Swords, the Five of Pentacles, and the Moon signify in the areas of friendship and romance?

Q6 How should Strength, the Chariot, and the Seven of Cups in position five be interpreted in relation to the cards in Question 5?

Q7 If the Devil, the Two of Swords, and the Ten of Swords appeared in position three, how would you assess the querent's chances of a happy love life?

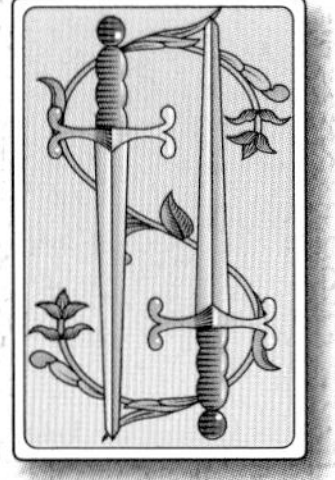
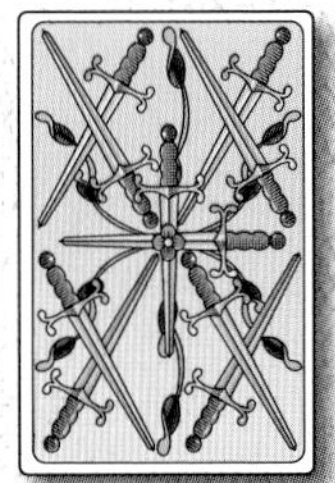

Q8 How would you evaluate the effect of the Lovers, the Chariot and the Queen of Cups in position five on the cards described in Question 7?

Q9 What significance do the Five of Swords, Temperance, and the Hanged Man in position three have for romance?

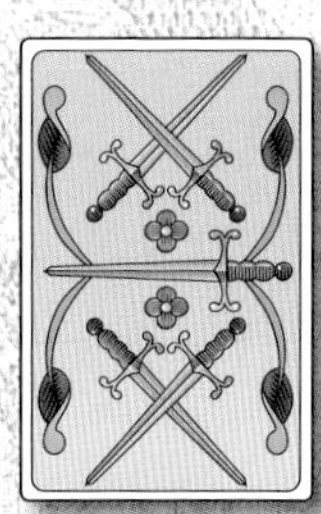

Q10 What does the combination of the Two of Swords, the Ten of Wands, and the Eight of Cups in position five mean, and how should they be interpreted in relation to Question 9?

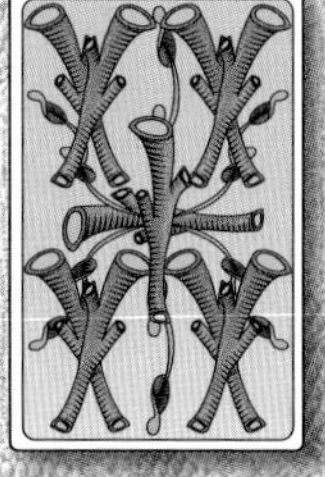

LOVE AND THE UNEXPECTED ANSWERS

A1 The Eight of Swords means indecision caused by negativity, lack of confidence, hypocrisy, and self-deception. However, when favorably aspected, as it is here with the Star, it represents new self-confidence, progress made, and hurts healed. The Star is a positive card symbolizing refreshment of the mind and spirit coming after a troubled period, spiritual strength and guidance, and unselfish help and encouragement given by loving friends, all of which will result in hope, inspiration, and renewed effort. The Seven of Pentacles signifies that a change is coming or that efforts from the past are about to bear fruit. So when these cards appear in position three, friendship and romance, they reveal that the querent is a creative and spiritual person but has possibly behaved badly to others in the past, done careless work, been made to feel inferior, or suffered emotionally. However, hurts will soon be healed and good friends are there to encourage, guide, and advise the querent. There may also be a new love coming into his or her life.

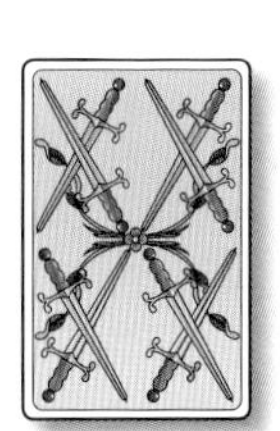

A2 The Chariot represents the controlling of animal passions, the balancing of positive and negative forces, triumphing over stress and problems, patience, sudden news, and sustained effort bringing wealth and prestige. The Tower can indicate a sudden change of life's pattern that ultimately brings happiness, illusions shattered, selfish ambitions destroyed, or a flash of inspiration that is the beginning of enlightenment. The Ace of Cups signifies a new love affair and joy in artistic work as well as spiritual nourishment, happy company, and good news. So this combination in position five, the unexpected, underlines the meaning of the cards in Answer 1, and reveals that, after the querent's emotional hurt, there will be inner enlightenment, spiritual strength, and a determination to produce careful and consistent work. There will also be triumph over stress and worries, good news that brings a beneficial change, true friends, joy in artistic work that earns prestige and wealth, and a new love affair.

A3 The Ace of Swords indicates that an inevitable occurrence will take place that is a strong force for good or ill, and it will change the querent's entire outlook. It can also mean strength in adversity, a conquest, triumph over obstacles, and carries with it a sense of the inevitable. However, this is not negative in position three, friendship and romance. The Queen of Cups represents the beloved wife or mistress, romantic, intuitive, sensitive, sociable, gifted artistically, and possibly new horizons bringing a new romance. The Four of Cups reveals that the querent is discontented and will undergo self-examination before searching for a new career. There is a warning here that other people's jealousy will ruin a new friendship or romance unless the querent listens to his or her inner voice or intuition. So, happily, the cards show that life will change through travel or starting a different career, and the querent will find real love as long as he or she does not listen to other people who are envious.

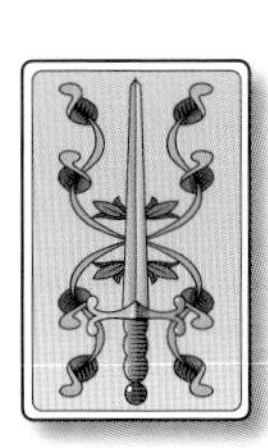

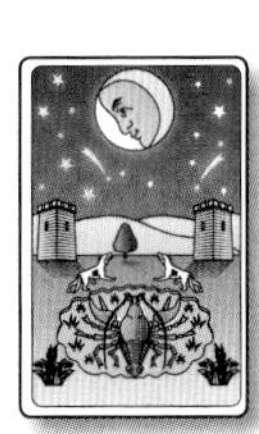

A4 These cards in position five, the unexpected, strengthen the warning given by the cards in Answer 3, for the Moon's meanings, such as hidden forces, deception, and an emotional crisis, are underlined here because the Moon followed by Justice denotes false accusations or slander. Fortunately, the Two of Cups comes after them, meaning a love affair, deep understanding, and spirituality creating a permanent bond and, happily, a reconciliation. So the querent will trust his or her own inner voice and all will be well.

A5 The Queen of Swords carries connotations of sorrow, privation, and a struggle between spiritual and material values. It can also represent a strong, self-reliant, intelligent, and cautious woman or widow, a good friend, a foreigner, or a foreign nation. When negatively aspected, as here, this person can be intolerant, spiteful, and a bad enemy. The Five of Pentacles symbolizes loss of judgment caused by emotions ruling the mind, loss of position, sorrow and disappointment, enforced restrictions, spiritual loneliness, and what is relevant in this position, loss of home, lover, or partner. However, it also has the positive meaning that lasting friendships will be made with those in similar circumstances. The Moon, signifying imagination, hidden forces, deception, occult power, the subconscious, creativity, mystery, dreams, uncertainty, deception, an emotional crisis, and a loved one's misfortune or illness, is not a positive influence in position three, friendship and romance. It is possible that the querent could be foreign or has married a foreigner, and unfortunately there may be a separation.

A6 Strength is the strongest and most positive card in the deck. It represents spiritual strength and triumph, courage, hate conquered by love, the mind's domination over material trials, and an opportunity that comes only once in a lifetime and that must be taken. Followed by the Chariot in position five, the unexpected, it means a triumph after sustained effort. The Chariot indicates that, after a period of stress and difficulty, the balancing of positive and negative forces will achieve triumphant success as well as patience, prestige, wealth, sudden news, and fast travel. The Seven of Cups symbolizes an unexpected offer requiring the right choice in order to make a dream come true. It also means mental ability, mystical experiences, and creative efforts bringing unexpected success. However, it carries a warning that the querent could become "Jack of all trades, master of none." So the strongest tarot card precedes two cards denoting physical and spiritual strength, courage, negativity vanquished, news, and the opportunity of a lifetime bringing surprising rewards. So the trouble and sad loss emanating from the cards in Answer 5 are transformed by strength, courage, and patience that will bring recovery for the lover or partner. The querent will also be offered a wonderful opportunity that needs the right choice and sustained effort to make a dream come true.

The Two of Swords is an unwelcome card in position three, friendship and romance, since it indicates stalemate and difficult choices. It reveals that the querent is confused about the best move to make.

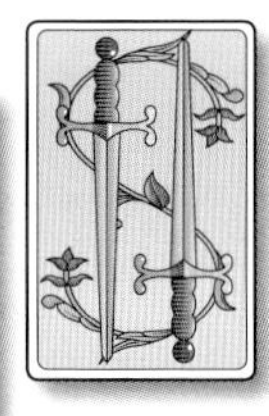
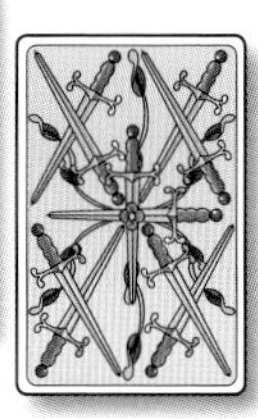

A7 The Devil, the most negative card in the Major Arcana, can influence all those close to it. It means negative power and attitudes based on fear, violence, superstition, greed, and ignorance, a life ruled by the physical senses, and the love of material gain. It also signifies a sudden inexorable event that, according to the cards around it, is either positive or negative. The Two of Swords can mean a stalemate, balanced forces, friendship in adversity, a sense of equilibrium, good coming out of evil, and spiritual peace and satisfaction after a difficult choice. Since it is badly aspected here, it also means indecision, self-deception, living in the past, and false pride causing a wrong choice. The Ten of Swords, the most negative Minor Arcana card, means the lowest point in the national economy or a personal affair, misfortune, and pain. Since these cards appear in position three, friendship and romance, the querent must be advised to make the right decision about an emotional problem to avoid pain and suffering. If this advice is not followed, and this is often the case, the result will be one of life's major lessons that eventually will bring self-honesty, self-acceptance, the end of spiritual darkness, and a spiritual rebirth.

A8 Although these cards in position five, the unexpected, seem at first glance to mean victory in love, unfortunately when the Lovers precedes the Chariot it signifies a shocking discovery of betrayal in an emotional affair. The Queen of Cups could stand for the querent if female, or the loved one, and usually means beloved wife or a new romance. However, if badly aspected as it is here, it is evident that the querent's relationship has been based on dishonesty. Although painful, this will teach a valuable lesson and bring eventual peace.

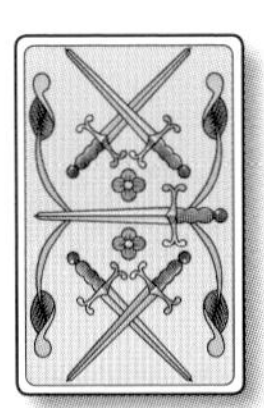

A9 The Five of Swords denotes that false pride must be recognized and personal limitations accepted before choosing a new direction. When badly aspected, it also signifies fear, humiliation, and defeat. Temperance, a positive card, represents a balanced attitude, peace, and harmony, while the Hanged Man means suffering, loss, sacrifice, and forgiveness bringing spiritual peace. However, when Temperance precedes the Hanged Man, it signifies indecision or hypocrisy through false promises. Since these cards are in position three, friendship and romance, it is possible that the querent has been deceived by a lover, but also self-deception could have been a major factor in an emotional relationship.

A10 In position five, the unexpected, the Two of Swords indicates a difficult decision that must be made. The Ten of Wands signifies that problems will soon be solved, and the solution could involve a journey. The Eight of Cups is a card of spiritual change brought about by suffering. So the querent must face some hard choices, but if he or she learn from past mistakes, a happier romantic future could be on the horizon.

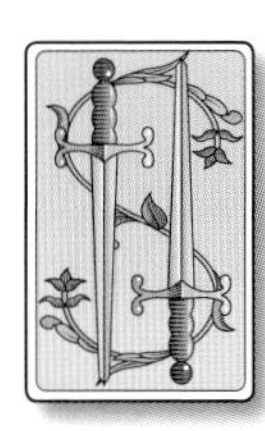
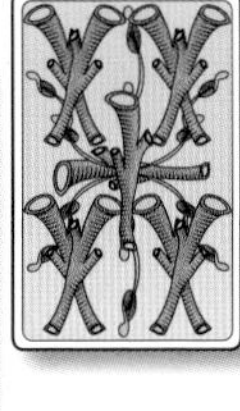

The Five of Swords in position three emphasizes that the querent must reflect on life and accept personal limitations if he or she is to develop rewarding relationships in the future.

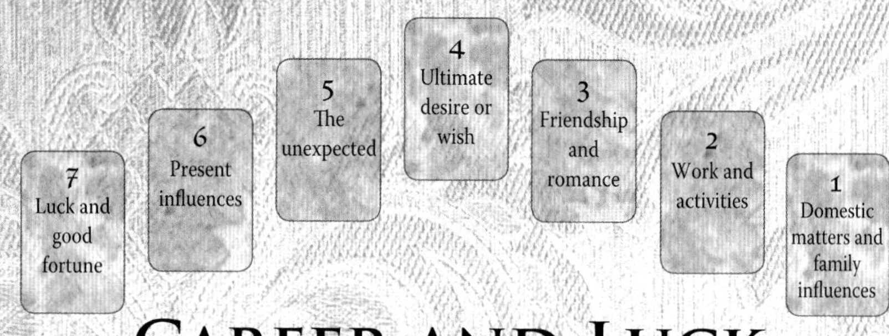

Career and Luck Questions

These questions look at the cards in position two, work and activities, and then examine how the cards in position seven, luck and good fortune, affect them. Refer to page 18-19 for instructions on how to do the Bohemian Spread; see pages 60-65 for the answers to these questions.

Q1 In position two, what do the Three of Pentacles, the Chariot, and the World indicate will happen in the querent's career?

Q2 If Strength, the Tower, and the Four of Wands appear in position seven, would they confirm, negate, or alter the meanings of the cards in Question 1?

Q3 What does the combination of the Ace of Wands, the King of Wands, and the Nine of Pentacles mean in position two?

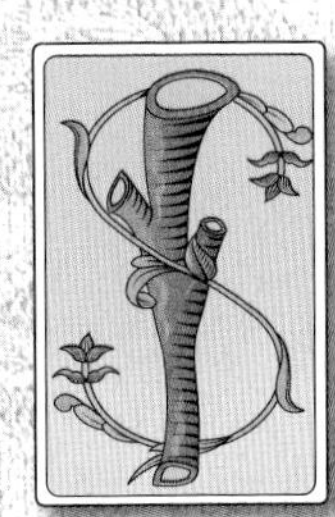

Q4 Bearing in mind the cards in Question 3, what interpretation would you give for the Knight of Cups, the Lovers, and the Magician in position seven?

Q5 Do the Four of Pentacles, the Devil, and the King of Swords in position two bode well for the querent's professional activities?

Q6 How will the Five of Wands, the Five of Pentacles, and Justice in position seven affect the cards in Question 5 in all matters concerning the querent's business interests?

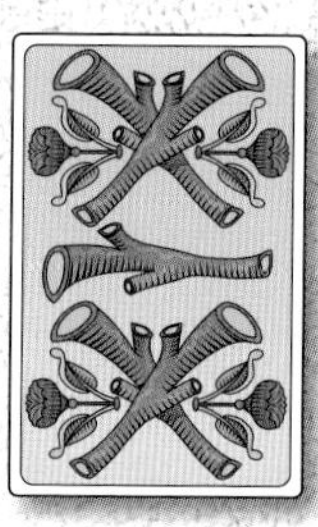

Q7 What meaning would you give for the Five of Cups, Temperance, and the Emperor in position two?

Q8 Assess the meaning of the Two of Wands, the Magician, and the Wheel of Fortune in position seven. How would they affect the cards listed in Question 7?

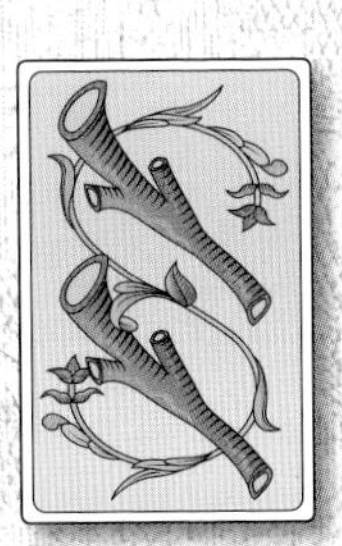

Q9 Are the Five of Pentacles, the Fool, and the Three of Wands in position two a good or bad omen for the querent's career prospects?

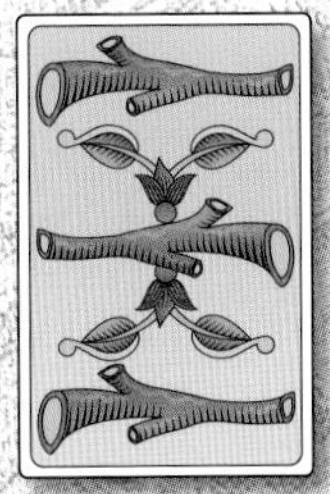

Q10 What evaluation would you give for the Five of Swords, the Hermit, and the Nine of Wands in position seven, and how will they affect the cards described in Question 9?

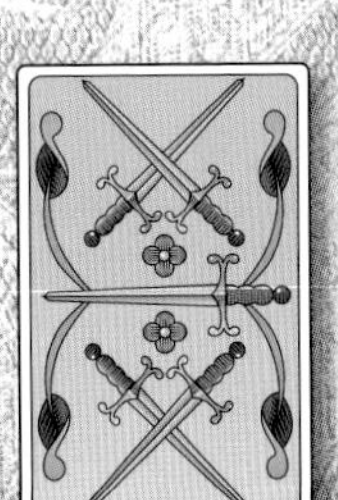

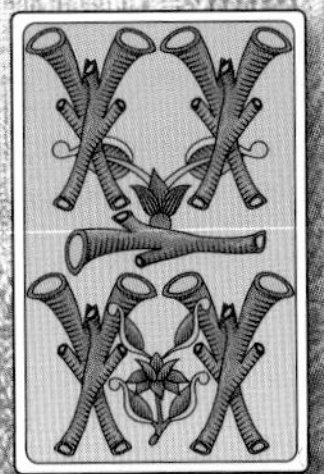

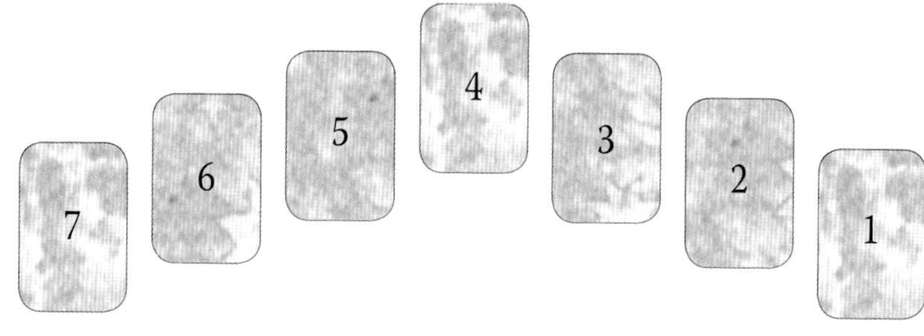

Career and Luck Answers

A1 The Three of Pentacles is the card of the professional or craftsperson. In position two, work and activities, it signifies that training, hard work, and consistent effort bring recognition and success. It also denotes that now is the time for successful expansion. The Chariot indicates that sustained effort will bring success and triumph, patience and endurance will lead to victory over stress or difficulties, and prestige, wealth, and sudden news or travel is on the horizon. The World, the material wish card, symbolizes spiritual and material success, the end of a cycle of life, long-distance travel, joy, a happy conclusion, and dreams coming true. When the Chariot comes before the World, it reveals that ambitions will be realized. These cards almost echo one another in their meanings. The querent has obviously worked hard to perfect a talent or skill, conquered stress, and triumphed over problems. There will be help, financial benefits, and cooperation from others that will bring honor, prestige, and wealth. There may also be an opportunity to expand a new business or to travel to another country.

A2 Strength represents the triumph of positive forces over negative. The Tower has negative connotations but in this example is between two positive cards, so it can only mean a flash of inspiration or enlightenment. The Four of Wands symbolizes perfected work, a journey away from home, and the gathering of the harvest after long labor. These cards in position seven, luck and good fortune, therefore reinforce those in Answer 1. They indicate that the querent may face a problem but will certainly overcome it and reap many rewards. The possibility of travel is also echoed.

A3 The Ace of Wands symbolizes new beginnings, artistic inspiration, creativity, and new knowledge and wisdom. It also represents dissatisfaction with present attitudes or circumstances, and the founding of a fortune or family. The King of Wands is a man over 35, intelligent, enthusiastic, generous, honest, and courageous, who is a born leader, gives wise advice, and could be successful in almost all creative, professional, or financial fields. This card can also mean a successful business or an unexpected inheritance. The Nine of Pentacles signifies a uniquely talented person who must learn that self-knowledge brings satisfaction and inner peace. It also means that sound administration and consistent effort or a successfully completed project will result in a substantial reward and sometimes solve a problem. This is a positive combination for position two, work and activities, revealing that the querent will be given help and advice by a wise and powerful man. If the querent is over 35, then it means that new knowledge brings a different direction or way of life, and wealth and success if this richly talented person works hard.

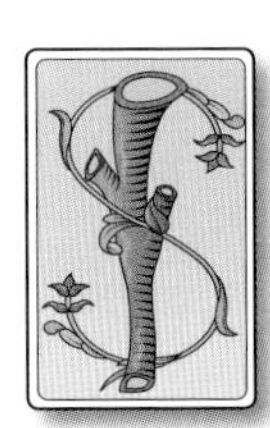

A4 The Knight of Cups, a man between 21 and 35, could represent a friend, rival, or lover or a fated relationship that teaches a lesson. The Lovers symbolizes intuitive decisions and a moment of choice, such as a moral dilemma between love and career. The Magician signifies willpower turning thought into action, new opportunities to use talents, and new beginnings. The Magician in conjunction with the Lovers implies indecision in commencing new projects or artistic ventures. In position seven, luck and good fortune, they reveal that a new unhappy love affair delays the start of a new venture, and although the querent may have to make a choice between career and love, it is more likely that the love affair will bring sadness through a lack of spiritual love or sincerity. This will cause a delay in starting a new life, but a lesson will be learned that results in self-knowledge and peace.

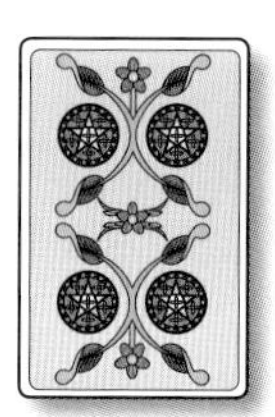

A5 The Four of Pentacles is the card of finance. It indicates financial stability, material security, acquisitiveness, the love of possessions, benefits and problems connected with finance, a legacy or inheritance, and the establishment of a commercial business or firm. Negatively aspected, as this is by the presence of the Devil, it means business problems, miserliness, and low self-esteem. The Devil, the strongest negative card in the tarot, denotes negative power and influences such as greed, violence, insensitivity, ignorance, fear, superstition, a life dominated by carnal desires and materialism, upheavals, and an inexorable event that can be either positive or negative, depending upon the surrounding cards. The King of Swords, also negatively aspected by the Devil, can be a cruel, violent, vengeful, or severe critic, possibly a lawyer or other professional. The Devil stands for greed and materialism, and when next to the card of finance in position two, work and activities, it implies business problems and failure as a result of a critical judgment from a government official or lawyer.

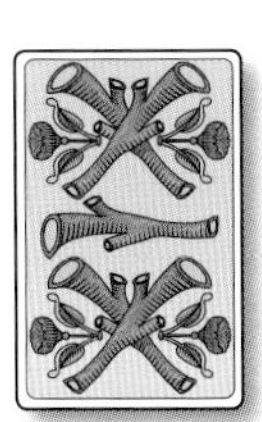

A6 The Five of Wands in position seven, luck and good fortune, signifies triumph over obstacles or a determined struggle overcoming material adversity. The Five of Pentacles can mean loss of judgment, loss of position or work, loss of a home or lover, or enforced spiritual loneliness. Its happier meanings are that lasting friendships will be made with those in similar circumstances. Here, next to the positive Justice, it also signifies regaining of faith, self-confidence, and a new start. It seems that the querent's professional activities have been misjudged or finances wrongly assessed, possibly through his or her own lack of thought or carelessness.

A7 The Five of Cups symbolizes something ended and something new beginning, a new life about to start, new paths to explore, or the end of a love affair, and also sometimes an inheritance. It carries a warning that one's own spiritual needs must never be ignored. Temperance denotes a balanced attitude to life, inspiration, compromise, moderation, energy, vitality, good financial sense, and future peace and harmony. The Emperor represents the dominating male force, temporal power, intellectual power, logical thought and analysis, creative and mental activity, knowledge gained through experience, self-discipline, passion, romance, and wealth. These cards in position two, work and activities, show that the querent possesses a sensible and balanced attitude to life, has good financial sense, is intellectual and creative, has energy and vitality, has possibly parted from a lover, and could receive an inheritance. However, the main message here is that a new career is about to start and the querent will receive help from a man in authority. The outlook is one of wealth, romance, and a harmonious and peaceful future.

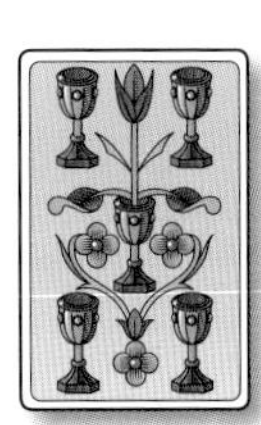

A8 These are good cards to have in position seven, luck and good fortune, for the Two of Wands echoes the meaning of the cards in Answer 7—consistent effort conquering problems, high motives, intellectual work, maturity won through tolerance, justice, help from people in high places, and strength and vision bringing lasting happiness and success. The Magician in this context could refer to the duality or union of personal and divine power, new beginnings, or new opportunities, while the Wheel of Fortune, in the context of its accompanying positive cards, must mean a beneficial change. Both the Wheel and the Magician can indicate a fortunate change of direction in profession or a change of residence. These cards therefore verify and strengthen the meaning of those in Answer 7.

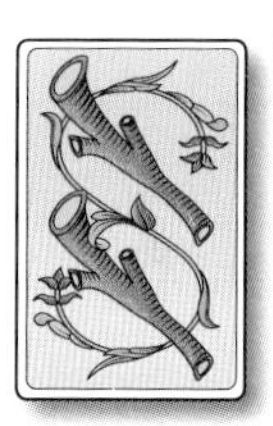

The Hermit in position seven, luck and good fortune, advises prudence when choosing a new but essential path in life.

A9 The Five of Pentacles means sorrow, disappointment, loss of position or business, loss of lover or home, and enforced restrictions. The positive aspect is that new friends are made who have had similar experiences. When near positive cards such as the Fool in position two, work and activities, it indicates that faith in self will be regained and a new start made. The Fool, a spiritual card, means self-development and spiritual progress as life's lessons are learned. The Three of Wands is another positive card and denotes an artist or inventor with powerful convictions and unusual power of expression, or the achievement of success through original or inspirational work. It can also indicate aid given by a powerful friend or a business partnership. It therefore seems that the querent will learn lessons and make important choices that bring spiritual strength and protection. So, although there will be some loss and disappointment, the querent's unique talents will bring eventual wealth and renown, possibly in partnership with a friend.

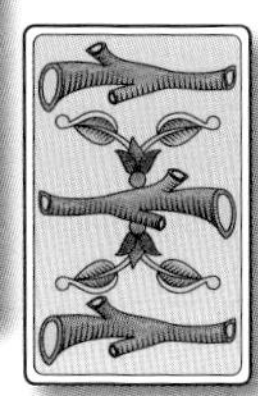

A10 The Five of Swords means recognizing false pride, acknowledging limitations, accepting the inevitable, facing defeat with courage before learning to build on secure foundations, and choosing a new direction in order to move onward and upward. The Hermit is the traveler or explorer, and indicates that caution is needed when choosing an unfamiliar but essential path. It also represents inner enlightenment coming from a journey, wise counsel given, sudden insight, and delayed achievement. The Nine of Wands, the strength card of the Minor Arcana, means sound advice given or taken, balanced judgment, and a victory after a final challenge. These cards in position seven, luck and good fortune, emphasize that if the querent learns from past mistakes and accepts wise counsel, success will eventually come.

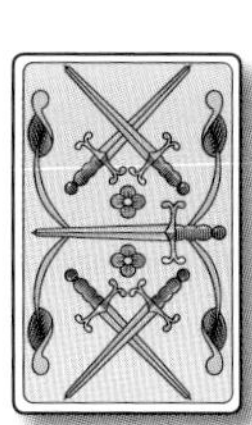

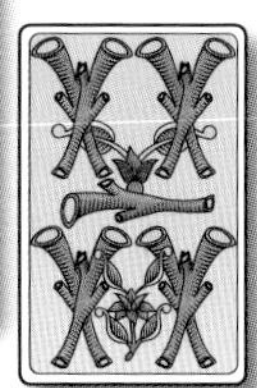

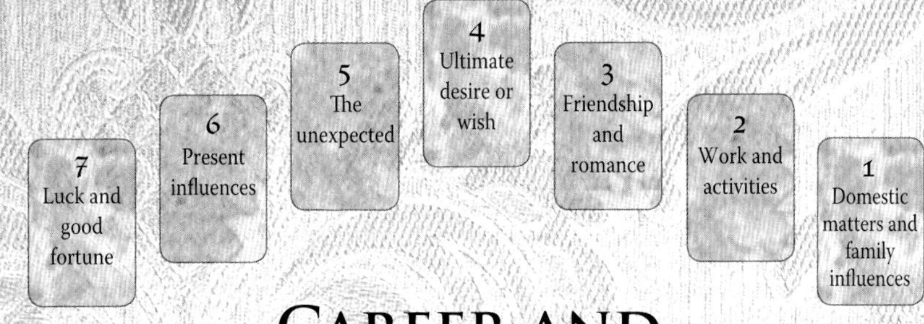

Career and Present Influences Questions

These questions look at the cards in position two, work and activities, and then examine how the cards in position six, present influences, affect them. Refer to page 18-19 for instructions on how to do the Bohemian Spread; see pages 70-75 for the answers to these questions.

Q1 In position two, what do the Magician, the Star, and the Six of Wands predict will happen in the querent's career or studies?

Q2 How would the Sun, Death, and the Ace of Wands in position six affect the cards in Question 1?

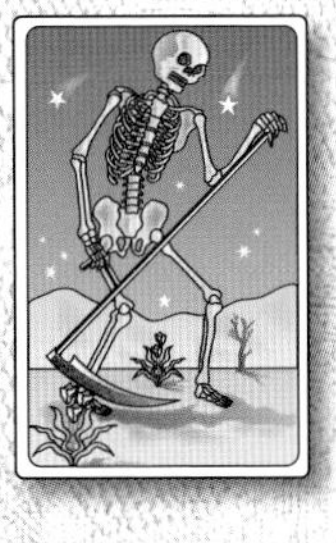
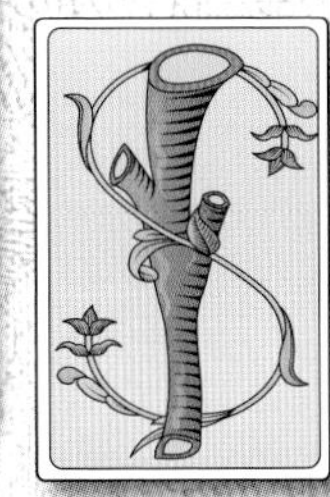

Q3 What does the combination of the Wheel of Fortune, the High Priestess, and the Ace of Swords mean in position two?

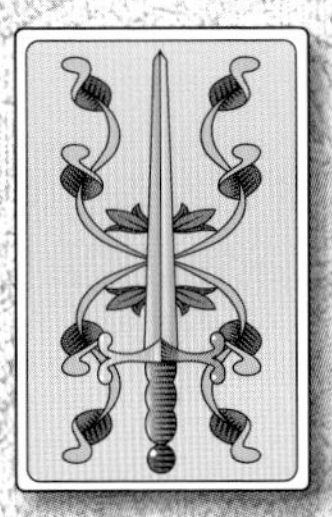

Q4 How would you evaluate the effect of Strength, Death, and the Four of Swords in position six on the cards described in Question 3?

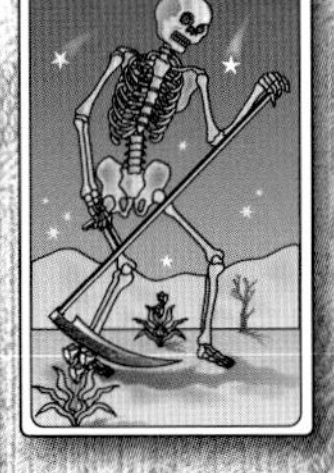
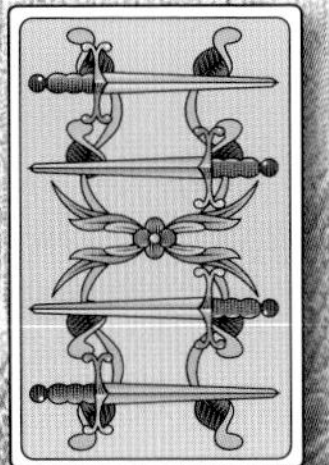

Q5 What meaning would you give for the Seven of Wands, the King of Pentacles, and the Sun in position two?

Q6 Keeping the cards in Question 5 in mind, how would you interpret the Two of Pentacles, the Wheel of Fortune, and the Magician in position six?

Q7 Do the High Priestess, Temperance, and the Nine of Wands in position two have positive or negative connotations for the querent's career?

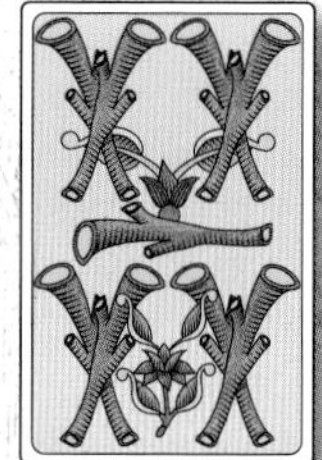

Q8 Consider the Moon, the Chariot, and the Knight of Swords in position six. How do you think they might clarify the meaning of the cards in Question 7?

Q9 If the Magician, the Wheel of Fortune, and the Eight of Pentacles appear in position two, what kind of career prospects would you foresee for the querent?

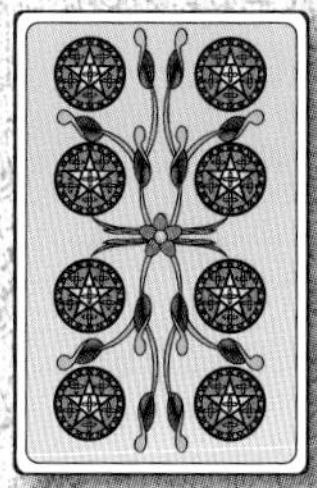

Q10 Would the Chariot, the Lovers, and the Queen of Swords in position six have any effect on the cards in Question 9?

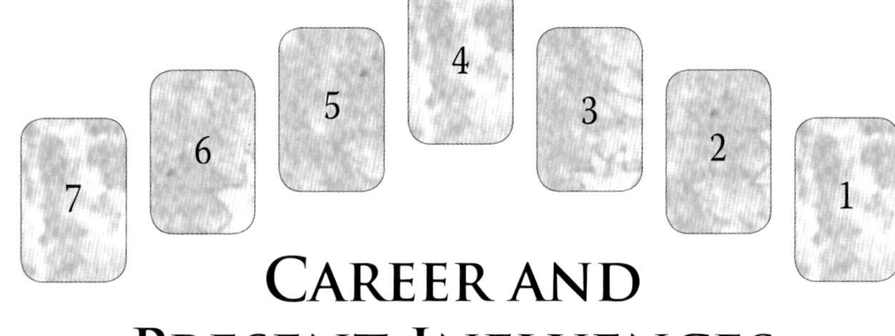

Career and Present Influences Answers

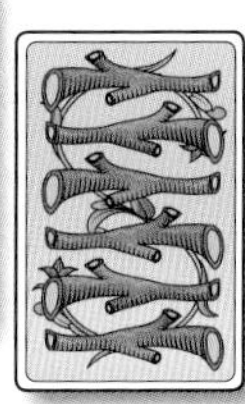

A1 The Magician is the commencement card, symbolizing new skills, searching for new beginnings, willpower turning thought into action, and skillful communication. It can also indicate guile and trickery, or the blending of personal power with divine power in a way that can be used selfishly. The Star means a refreshment of the mind and spirit after a period of darkness, resulting in spiritual strength. It also refers to guidance and unselfish help given by good friends that brings inspiration and hope and results in renewed effort. The Six of Wands is the career card of the Minor Arcana, signifying victory in a difficult situation, the solution to a major problem, diplomacy overcoming opposition, success coming after a struggle, wonderful news, a triumphant achievement in a career, the fulfillment of ambitions, great satisfaction, and public acclaim. However, it also warns that triumph will be soured by the envy of others. In position two, work and activities, the cards therefore show that the querent, after going through a sad and troubled time, has started or is about to commence a new career, or is about to complete unfinished or interrupted academic or artistic studies. Love, encouragement, and wise guidance will be given unselfishly by friends, which will ensure new self-confidence and renewed effort. The finished work brings great satisfaction and the fulfillment of ambition. The only warning is that envious people will try to spoil the querent's happiness.

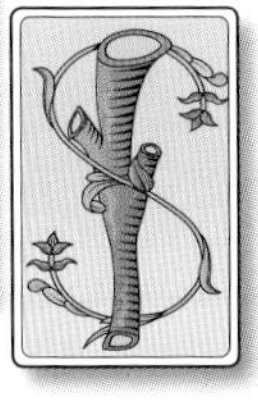

A2 The Sun in position six, present influences, means successful achievement in any field and against all odds, as well as completed studies, health, the end of self-deception, and the gift of gratitude. Death is a highly spiritual card that indicates the overturning of the old life and a soul reborn. The Ace of Wands means new beginnings, new creative activities, and the founding of a family or fortune. The Sun preceding Death signifies a positive end to something, such as the querent's struggles in a sad and troubled past through self-deception and lack of confidence. Dissatisfaction with present attitudes could also denote that the querent's new spiritual strength will conquer hurt, and he or she will be able to forgive the envy and spite of others that is predicted in Answer 1.

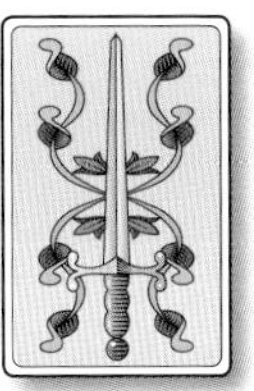

A3 The Wheel of Fortune followed by the High Priestess means success in arts, science, and literature. The Ace of Swords, meaning "you reap what you sow," can be negative if badly aspected, but here it is preceded by the positive Priestess. It therefore represents triumph over obstacles and something unstoppable bringing a new attitude to life. When the Ace is in position two, work and activities, it must mean that this new attitude leads to lasting professional success.

The Sun in position six, present influences, symbolizes the realization of goals and the completion of studies, giving the querent enough confidence to make a fresh start in life.

A4 Strength is the strongest and most positive card in the deck. If it comes after Death, it means an abrupt breaking of a pattern of life, but coming before Death as it does here, it denotes a serious illness but one that will not be fatal. With the Four of Swords, which represents hospitalization, convalescence, or a voluntary retreat to think things through, coming after both these cards in position six, present influences, it becomes obvious that the querent will be delayed in starting a career due to illness. This illness may not affect the querent directly; a parent, partner, or child could be the one involved. Since the meaning of the cards in Answer 3 were so positive, this would indicate that this setback is only temporary. The presence of Strength emphasizes this, so although the illness is serious, it is not fatal and the querent will certainly go on to fulfill professional ambitions.

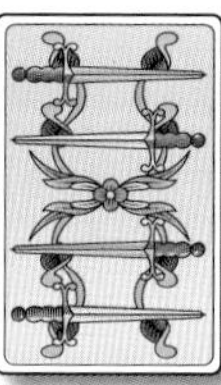

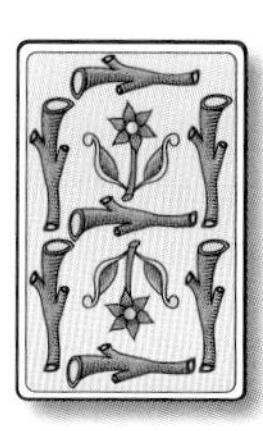

A5 The Seven of Wands denotes writing and disseminating knowledge. It signifies that inner strength and determination will ensure success, that opposition can only be defeated by courage and sustained effort, and also a change in profession. The King of Pentacles is a man over 35, patient, stable, with a deliberate mind, who can be inarticulate or uneducated yet possesses intuitive wisdom, an aptitude for mathematics, and is often connected with financial matters. He is a good parent but a bad enemy, and is loyally protective of friends. The Sun symbolizes harmonious relationships, the gift of gratitude, the end of self-deception, material comfort, health, energy, completed studies, and achievement in any field. In position two, work and activities, these cards show that the querent will be helped by the King of Pentacles, who is either a friend, adviser, or father, to change profession and become a writer, lecturer, or teacher. This is reinforced by the Seven of Wands, which always means learning to share or spread knowledge. The Sun indicates studies completed and ambitions realized.

A6 The Two of Pentacles means harmony and skill in a time of financial or domestic change, the use of one talent to bring success, literary ability, and sometimes a move to a new home or country. The Wheel of Fortune symbolizes a sudden change, usually as the result of past efforts, that sometimes brings problems but ones that will prove beneficial in time. The Magician represents turning thought into action, willpower, communication, and new skills. The meaning of the cards in Answer 5 is therefore reinforced by these cards in position six, present influences, but the Magician coming after the Wheel of Fortune indicates that a delay will occur. However, the querent will definitely experience triumph and joy in studies or work.

Writing and imparting knowledge is the rewarding destiny indicated by the Seven of Wands in position two, work and activities. It could also indicate that the querent may embark on a career change and become a teacher.

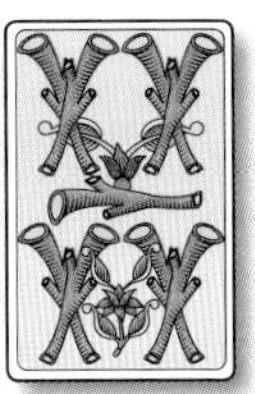

A7 The High Priestess brings protection, for it represents inner perception and spiritual enlightenment, as well as philosophy, silence, cultural advancement, creative ability, and the scholar who loves learning. Temperance combines the active with the passive to create a balanced attitude to life, and denotes moderation, compromise, good financial sense, peace, future harmony, and creative inspiration. The Nine of Wands, the most powerful card

in the Minor Arcana, indicates that strength and integrity bring a lasting triumph or a victory after a final challenge. It also symbolizes success and expansion in professional or artistic fields, sound advice given or taken, balanced judgment, strength in reserve, courage in defense, and an honest and trusting nature. In position two, work and activities, these cards reveal that, after consistent effort, the querent has achieved high standards in a professional, educational, or creative field, and through lessons already learned from life, possesses a balanced nature. It is therefore not surprising to see that, after a final challenge, there will be a lasting professional triumph as a result of ability, courage, strength, and integrity.

A8 The Moon can indicate an emotional crisis and a time of uncertainty and fluctuation. The Chariot sometimes denotes triumph over difficulties, but when it follows the Moon, it means illness or scandal. The Knight of Swords can suggest a conflict that must be faced, and when it is near cards denoting illness, it represents a surgeon. The cards in Answer 7 indicated that the querent would have to face a final challenge before going on to professional triumph, and the cards in position six, present influences, are clearly concerned with what this challenge will be. Since the Chariot is accompanied by the Moon and the Knight of Swords, it is obvious that it will be an illness and operation.

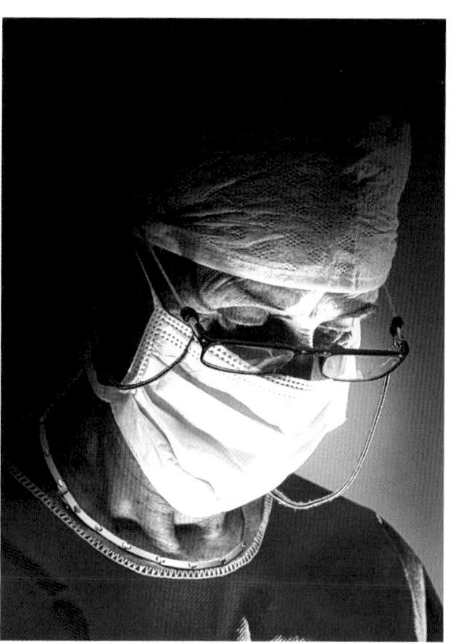

When the Knight of Swords appears near cards denoting illness, it represents a surgeon. In position six, present influences, this could mean a surgical operation is imminent.

A9 The Magician means new beginnings, turning thought into action, and skillful communication, but it also warns of trickery and that the combination of personal and divine power may be used selfishly. The Wheel of Fortune represents the law of retribution, a karmic lesson that ensures the gaining of wisdom and balance, or a sudden change as the result of past efforts that brings problems and setbacks but that in time proves fortunate. The Eight of Pentacles denotes a creative or artistic talent recently developed through energy and determination that has become a profession. It also signifies hard work rewarded or success in a skilled field bringing future financial gains. However, if the Wheel is opposite or beside the Magician as it is here in position two, work and activities, it means a delay will occur, probably through the problems or setbacks that come with the Wheel. These will cause a delay at the start of the querent's new career, but will ultimately bring success and wealth.

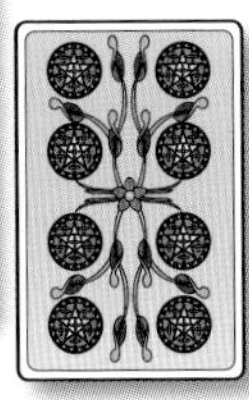

A10 The Chariot coming before the Lovers indicates that a sudden departure will stop a project. However, the Chariot also means that there will be a triumph, while the Lovers foretell that an emotional choice will be made. The Queen of Swords, coming after the Lovers, could mean a dark-haired lover, friend, or a foreign country. These cards in position six, present influences, show that the delay alluded to by the cards in Answer 9 involves a difficult choice that the querent will have to make. However, the delay will not affect the ultimate success.

The Magician in position two, work and activities, shows that the querent is a skilled communicator who will achieve professional success. However, it also warns of trickery and the selfish use of power.

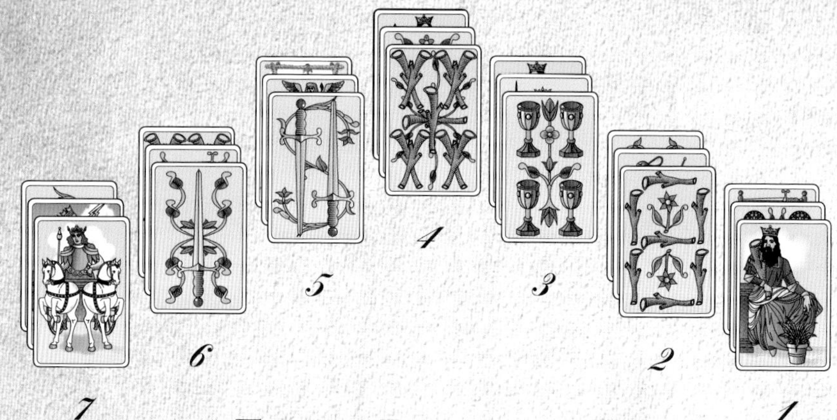

FULL READING

This is an example of a full reading using the Bohemian Spread (see page 18-19 for instructions). Remember to start the reading at position four, then look at positions five, six, and seven before returning to the beginning and assessing the cards in positions one, two, and three.

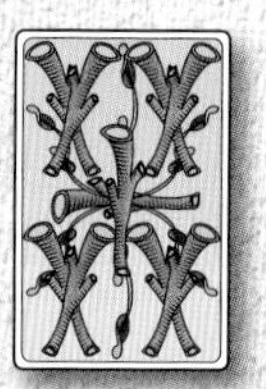

4: Ultimate Desire or Wish

The Ten of Wands symbolizes burdens soon to be lifted, problems solved, discarding fixed ideas in order to progress in a new direction, new ventures, big business, and an overseas trip. The Four of Pentacles is the card of finance, denoting material and financial stability, financial benefits and problems, the establishment of a commercial firm or business, acquisitiveness, love of possessions, a legacy, or an inheritance. The Queen of Swords can represent a strong woman who makes a good friend but a bad enemy, a struggle between spiritual and material values, or a foreign woman or foreign country. So it seems the querent loves money and possessions, and wishes to succeed in a new type of business that could possibly be connected with a foreign country.

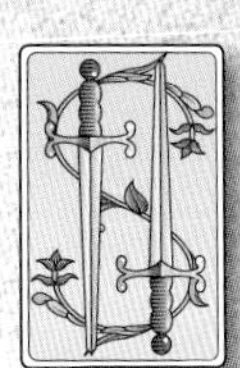

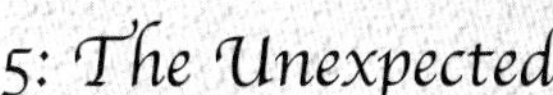
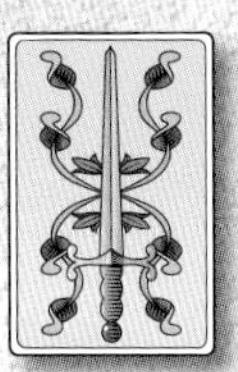
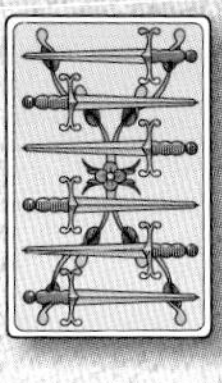

5: The Unexpected

The Two of Swords is the card of balanced forces, stalemate, equilibrium, good coming out of evil, adversity bringing help and friendship, and spiritual peace and satisfaction resulting from a difficult choice. The Wheel of Fortune symbolizes the law of retribution or karma, evolution bringing wisdom and balance, and capricious fate. It can also indicate a sudden change, sometimes as a result of past efforts, that may initially create problems or setbacks but will prove beneficial in time. The Hanged Man is a highly spiritual card that denotes loss, hardship, sacrifice, a decision that leads to spiritual peace, forgiveness bringing peace and wisdom, occult power, inner strength, and the reversal of a way of life. These three cards seem to show that the querent will suddenly decide to change his or her life, possibly through a lesson learned that will bring peace and joy.

6: Present Influences

The Ace of Swords is the card of divine justice and denotes a conquest, a strong sense of the inevitable, or a strong force for good or evil. It is something that cannot be stopped but that will change the querent's perspective on life. It also represents strength in adversity and triumph over obstacles. The Six of Swords is the card of flight or travel and signifies a change to a better environment, a change of work, success after anxiety, good news brought by someone from overseas, and obstacles removed. The Eight of Wands is the card of movement, speed, and haste in travel, a sudden air journey, overseas connections, unexpected news arriving suddenly, the end of a delay or period of quiet, and sudden changes that bring progress. It also indicates that it is time for the querent to try something new. So after facing troubles courageously and making a difficult decision, it seems that the querent will travel to another place and achieve success.

7: Luck and Good Fortune

The Chariot denotes patience and endurance bringing triumph over difficulties and stress. It also indicates success, wealth, and prestige after sustained effort, fast travel, and sudden news. The Tower can mean a sudden shock, the death of selfish ambitions, the shattering of illusions, but also a change or disruption of life's pattern, usually for the better, or a flash of inspiration that brings enlightenment. This last meaning could be particularly relevant here, since the Two of Pentacles denotes rewards gained by the development and use of one talent, and literary ability. It also signifies a journey to a new home or country.

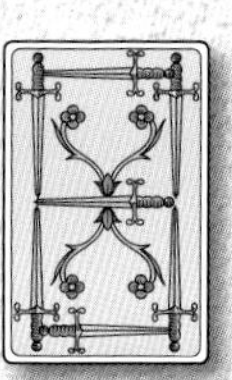

1: Domestic Matters and Family Influences

The King of Wands could represent the querent if male, or a relative or friend who is honest, generous, courageous, and intelligent. This person could be successful in a professional, financial, or creative field. He is sympathetic and gives wise counsel. This card can also mean an unexpected inheritance or a new business. The Eight of Pentacles is the talent or energy card of the tarot and signifies that professional changes are coming from a recently developed skill. The Seven of Swords is not a negative card but it does carry the warnings that greed can affect principles, aggressive methods will bring disaster, and the querent must use brain rather than brawn. It also advises that prudence, foresight, cunning, and evasion could be needed to avoid an obstacle or solve a problem. So it is evident that there will be success through work and possibly the start of a highly profitable new business or profession. However, the querent is warned that love of money could result in greed and the loss of moral principles.

2: Work and Activities

The Seven of Wands is the teacher's card and means lecturing, writing, and the dissemination of knowledge. It also indicates that sustained effort and courage will be needed to defeat opposition, and inner strength and determination will lead to success and a change of profession. The Magician is the commencement card, meaning new beginnings and new opportunities, a new use of talent, skillful communication, and willpower that turns thought into action. The Three of Pentacles echoes a little of what the Eight of Pentacles says in position one, for it is the card of professionalism and craftsmanship. It carries the message that training and hard work will lead to success, honor, and recognition. It symbolizes a skilled trade or artistic ability, help or cooperation from others, and financial rewards, and denotes that the time is right for a successful expansion in business. So it is evident that the querent is working hard and thinking of starting a business that could be successful.

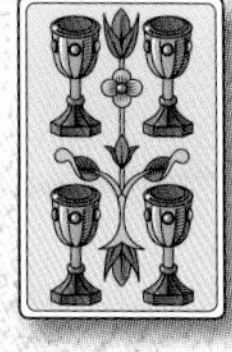

3: Friendship and Romance

The Four of Cups shows that the querent is discontented with his or her present life and this will lead to a period of self-examination resulting in a search for a new direction in life and a change of career. It also warns that a new love affair or friendship could be ruined by jealousy or hostility from others and advises the querent to listen always to his or her own inner voice. Justice can symbolize a balanced outlook, successful combinations, honesty, integrity, or a positive outcome from legal or educational disputes. The Queen of Cups is a romantic card representing the beloved wife or mistress as well as new horizons and new romance. So it is obvious that the querent will make a positive career change. However, there is a warning that a budding romance could be ruined if the querent allows him or herself to be swayed by the opinions of others who are jealous.

The Queen of Cups is a romantic card representing the beloved wife or mistress as well as new horizons and romance.

Interpretation

The message that comes through in this reading is that the querent is dissatisfied with his or her current life, work, or studies. There will be a time of suffering or trouble that will cause the querent to reevaluate his or her life and this will require courage and self-honesty. The querent will then experience a flash of inspiration and will make a difficult choice that leads to a new beginning. It is possible that one specific talent will be used, perhaps more, and the querent will have to work hard and consistently in a new profession, or start a new business that may have contacts with another country. Whatever the case, the result will be success, happiness, and reward. There will also be a romance that may be connected with a foreign country. This has the potential to become a happy long-term partnership as long as the querent learns to trust inner feelings or intuition and does not listen to jealous and destructive people. The only other warning is that the querent should not place too much importance on money.

The cards in this reading show that the querent is dissatisfied with his or her work or studies. The Seven of Wands—the teacher's card—in position two could indicate a career change related to teaching.

The Romany Draw

The Romany Draw is traditionally used to answer a specific question. Although this spread only uses three cards, it is deceptively difficult because three cards do not always supply sufficient information. You may therefore have to perform this spread up to three times to find the answer to a question. Sample questions that a querent may ask have been devised and organized into four subjects—love, career, health, and personal character. A full reading that takes all these subjects into account is described at the end of the chapter.

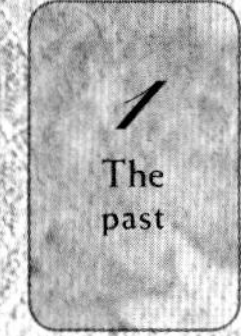

LOVE AND ROMANCE QUESTIONS

Refer to page 20-21 for instructions on how to perform the Romany Draw; see pages 88-93 for the answers to these questions.

Q1 "I was shocked to discover my lover was stealing cars. When he left he said I expected too much of others, and would never find an honest man. Will I?"

Q2 "I met a man at a party last week and I felt he and I were soulmates. We talked all night and he said he'd phone but he hasn't. Should I phone him?"

Q3 "I have been offered a wonderful promotion, but it would mean moving a great distance and my wife doesn't want to leave her mother, who lives alone. What can I do to change her mind?"

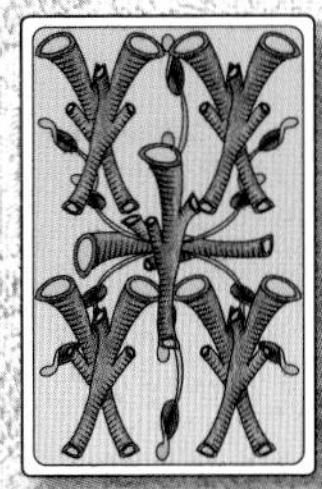

Q4 "Last week I retired from teaching and am receiving money from an insurance fund. I want to rent a cabin in a quiet area and write a book on modern education. My wife wants to take a world tour and says I'm selfish. Am I?"

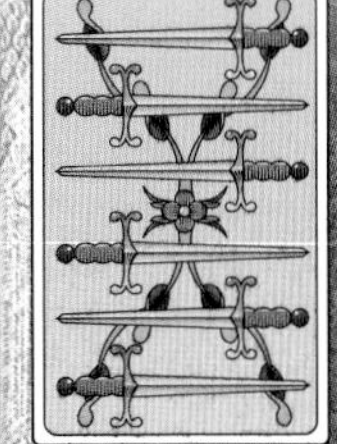

Q5 "The man I love has returned to his homeland to attend a university there. Will he send for me as he promised, and marry me?"

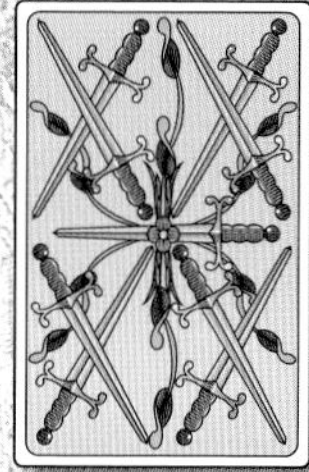
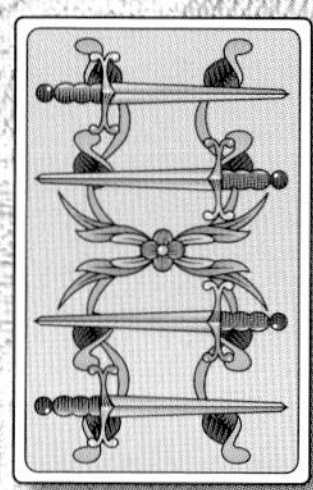
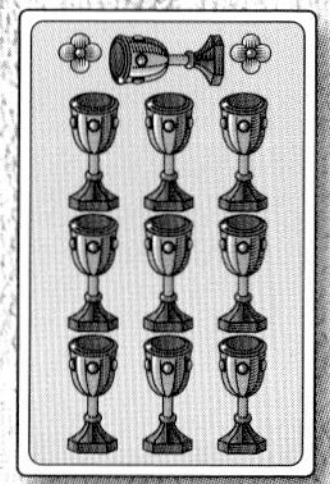

Q6 "I've fallen for a man who just kisses me goodbye at the door after we've been out together. I feel he is deeply attracted to me. Am I wrong?"

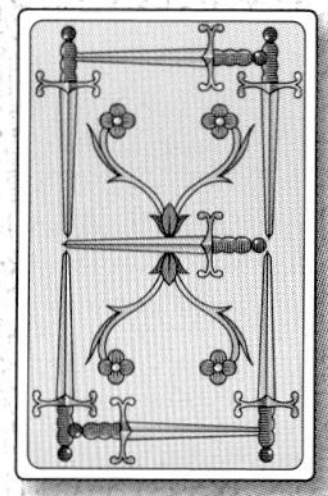

Q7 "I've discovered my partner has been having an affair with my best friend. I feel so hurt and betrayed. What am I going to do?"

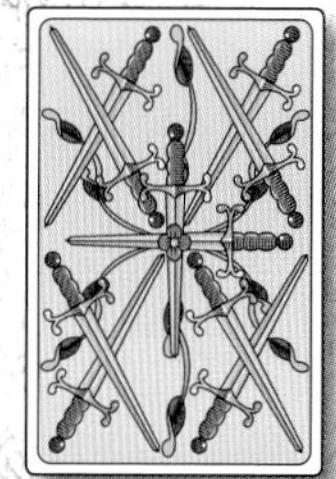

Q8 "I met the woman I want to marry, but she is divorcing her husband and says she will never marry or live with another man. Will she change her mind?"

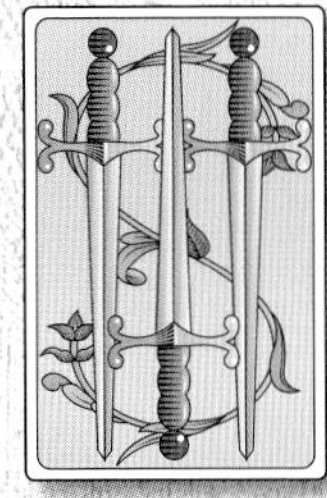

Q9 "My long relationship with a married man is finished because he was elected to a government office. Will I meet someone who will treat me better?"

Q10 "My boyfriend and I were together for four years, but he moved out overnight because I said I wanted to get married. Will he come back? I love him."

LOVE AND ROMANCE ANSWERS

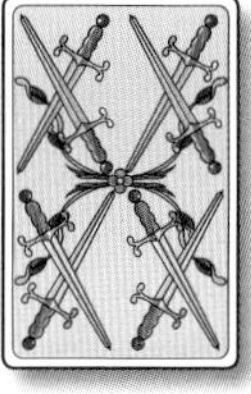

When difficulties occur in life, it is important to keep in contact with friends who can give advice without judgment. The presence of the Star shows that friends will give plenty of support.

A1 The Moon in the past indicates hidden forces, deception, and an emotional crisis. The Eight of Swords in the present means that patience, self-honesty, and confidence are needed to change the status quo and to avoid hurt from others. When favorably aspected with a positive Major Arcana card in the future position, as it is in this instance, the Eight of Swords also signifies that hurts will be healed, self-confidence regained, and progress made. The Star symbolizes hope, love, rebirth, a spirit refreshed and strengthened, and

optimism regained after a dark period in life. It also carries the message that the querent has many good friends who will offer help and support through this time of trouble because of the querent's loving and positive nature.

A2 The Knight of Cups in the past could represent a lover who is intelligent, romantic, a little egotistical, and sometimes devious and selfish. Temperance in the present symbolizes energy, creative genius, inspiration, peace, future harmony, the combination of the spiritual and the material, moderation, and a balanced attitude to life. It would therefore appear that the man in question is a person who knows his own mind and will act when he thinks the time is right. With the Ace of Cups in the future, which can denote a new love affair, and a marriage if combined with other romantic cards as it is in this example, the querent should be advised to take things slowly and to wait for him to call.

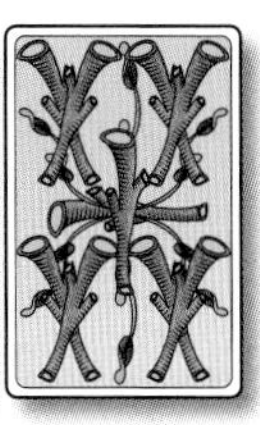

A3 The Wheel of Fortune in the past symbolizes destiny, cause and effect, wisdom from experience, a creative breakthrough, a new life, and wealth. It also indicates a sudden change, usually as a result of past efforts, that could create setbacks or difficulties at first, but that in time will prove to be beneficial. In respect to the querent's problem, Temperance in the present is one of the best cards to appear because it means peace, future harmony, the combination of the spiritual and the material, vitality, life, and creative inspiration. Perhaps more importantly here, it indicates moderation, good financial sense, and compromise. The Ten of Wands in the future, well-aspected next to Temperance, denotes new contracts or ventures, a journey to a strange place or an overseas trip, fixed ideas being abandoned in order to progress in a new direction, and burdens soon to be lifted. It is probable that the pair will decide to provide accommodation in their new location for the querent's mother-in-law, because Ten of Wands also means problems solved.

 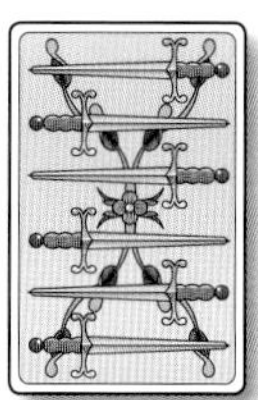 

A4 The presence of two Major Arcana cards in this three-card spread signifies that something very important will happen in the querent's life. Temperance in the past, apart from meaning the combination of the spiritual and the material, compromise, moderation, a balanced attitude to life (which must mean he is both a giving person and a born teacher), is also the symbol of vitality, energy, creative inspiration, and future peace and harmony. It is no surprise to see the Six of Swords in the present position. When badly aspected, it indicates that patience is necessary to solve a problem. Its other meanings—flight or travel to a better environment, a change of work and obstacles removed after a stressful period, the end of a difficult time coming, and risk bringing reward—imply that the teacher will go away to write a book he feels is necessary for society. With Justice in the future, symbolizing a positive result from educational or legal concerns, a balanced outlook, success, honesty, integrity, and the vindication of truth, it would appear that the book will bring to the querent both success and high honors in his field.

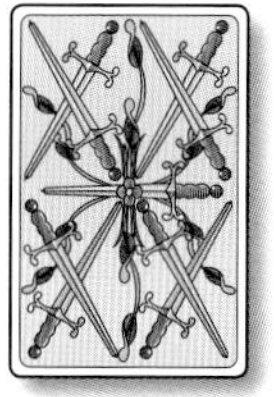 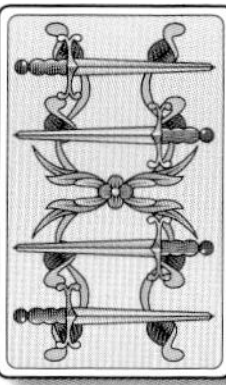 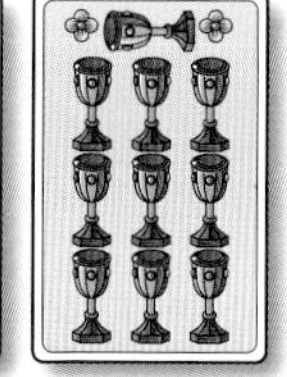

A5 The Nine of Swords in the past symbolizes suffering borne with patience and courage, a sense of isolation, loss, despair, a difficult choice entailing sacrifice, and sometimes the sad news of someone's accident or death. When positively aspected, it means time heals all wounds, shedding the past, and the beginning of a new, active, and rewarding life. The Four of Swords in the present can signify peace and order coming after struggle, or chaos in matters of administration, a hospitalization, or a voluntary retreat to think things through. When badly aspected, it indicates that diplomacy is needed or a decision must be postponed. In this instance, the two Sword cards together are negatively aspected, so they must refer to the sense of isolation and fear the querent feels and the fact that she must be tactful and allow her lover some space to work through his feelings. Luckily, the Ten of Cups in the future is one of the happiest cards in the deck. It represents deep and lasting spiritual peace, work in a public sphere, honor, prestige, a journey that results in happiness, successful legal matters regarding property and residence, and the love of friends. The cards therefore indicate that the querent must endure her feelings of loss, and if she is patient and diplomatic, her lover will indeed want her to join him in the future.

can mean that plans will go awry and progress will be inhibited. Happily, it is positively aspected in this spread by the Sun in the future, which represents courage, strength, joy, harmony, and success. However, the Sun can also indicate a childlike faith in the future, implying that the querent is sometimes too direct. The cards therefore indicate that if she remains her loving self but says nothing, is patient, and waits, the relationship will be happy.

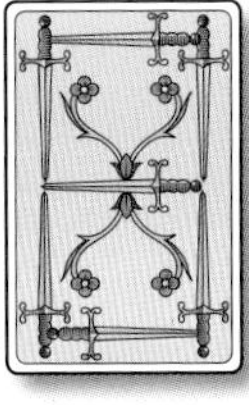

A6 The Three of Cups in the past represents the feminine element in nature, sensitivity to others, a capacity for giving, and a victorious conclusion. It also symbolizes emotional growth, love, and fulfillment in a partnership, friendship, or marriage. However, the Seven of Swords in the present can indicate that aggression will bring failure, and that prudence, foresight, evasion, and occasionally cunning are needed to solve a problem or to gain an objective. When badly aspected, it

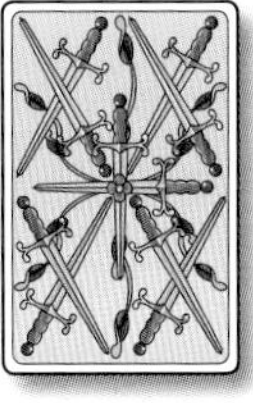

A7 The Moon in the past can indicate deception, uncertainty, and an emotional crisis, but its positive meaning is storms weathered. The Ten of Swords in the present represents the lowest point in human affairs, misfortune, and pain. However, its most important meaning in this particular spread is that, for the first time, something is being seen clearly for what it really is, not what it has seemed to be in the past, which must refer to the falsity of the querent's relationship with both partner and friend. Strength in the future is the strongest spiritual card in the deck and influences the entire reading positively. It symbolizes courage and power used wisely, love conquering hate, positive forces overpowering negative ones, and a wonderful, once-in-a-lifetime opportunity that will change the querent's future.

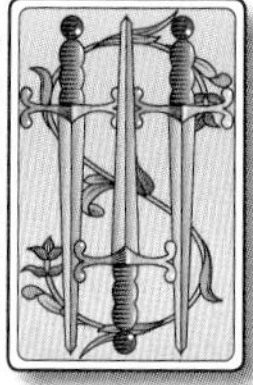

A8 The Queen of Wands has among her qualities generosity, tolerance, determination, and independence. However, if badly aspected next to a card such as the Three of Swords, as in this instance, the Queen can be bitter, narrow-minded, and judgmental, just as the woman in question is behaving at present. The Three of Swords can also indicate a permanent marital break-up, bringing pain followed by healing, and signify that the ground will be cleared for something better. It also means dwelling on old hurts. However, the Empress in the future is a card of abundance. She represents warm family life, femininity, intuition, protection, wealth, love, and happy marriage. It is therefore clear that the querent's lover has many positive qualities, and if given a little time to get over previous hurts and see things fairly, she and the querent could enjoy a happy marriage together.

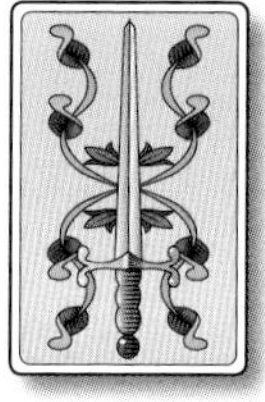
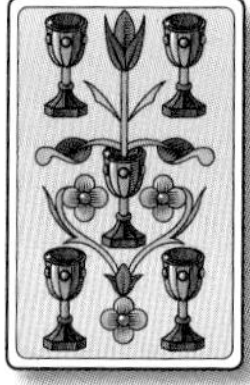

A9 The Ace of Swords in the past indicates a new beginning, perhaps referring to the man in question. It is also the card of divine justice and carries the adage "you reap what you sow." It indicates that an inexorable event has happened that will change the querent's attitude to life. When badly aspected, as it is when combined with the Five of Cups, it means disappointment, but followed by a victory. The Five of Cups indicates that a love affair is finished. There may be regret and concerns about past behavior or mistakes, but it is a warning that one's inner voice and spiritual needs must not be ignored. This is also strengthened by the more beneficial Six of Cups in the future, which gives a warning not to live in the past, but instead to learn from previous actions and mistakes, and use these lessons to influence future behavior in a positive way. It also indicates that a past love is coming back into the life of the querent, and this time her choice will be based on honesty and love.

When the Empress appears in a spread, the querent can be sure that a lover possesses many positive qualities. It is possible that the couple could share a happy marriage at some point in the future.

A10 The Tower in the past symbolizes an unexpected catastrophe, illusions shattered, a disruption of life's pattern, or the end of something. It dominates the other cards in the spread and clearly refers to the querent's relationship. Its other meaning, the beginning of enlightenment, could indicate that the querent will eventually realize that her boyfriend was afraid to commit and how different their views on life were. The Two of Cups in the present can sometimes mean reconciliation, but not in this case when it follows the Tower. Here, it signifies that emotion and spirituality will create a permanent bond or engagement. The Queen of Cups in the future represents a loving, idealistic, sensitive, intuitive, and beloved wife, denoting that the querent will be happily married in a true union. The presence of the Tower reveals that this marriage will be with a different person and will occur some time in the future.

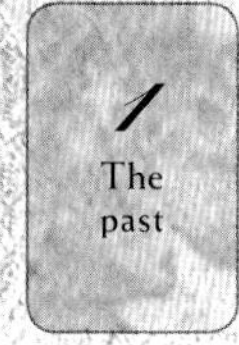

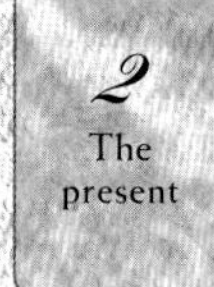

Career and Success Questions

Refer to page 20-21 for instructions on how to perform the Romany Draw; see pages 98-103 for the answers to these questions.

Q1 "I've worked as a farmer all my life but my business has been doing poorly for some time. My wife wants me to sell the farm and become a partner in her father's hotel business abroad. Should I take the step?"

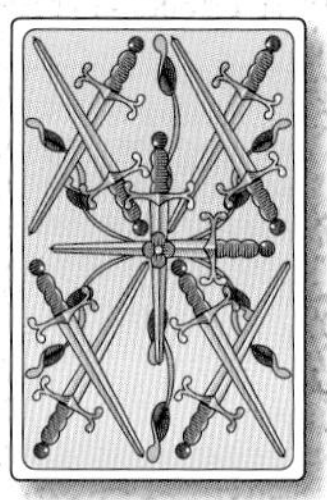

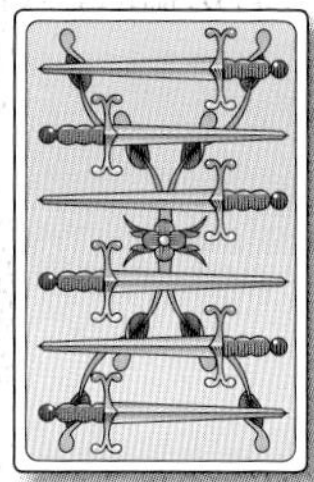

Q2 "My partner in a car rental business is twice my age and about to retire. He wants me to take out a loan and buy his share. I'm a mechanic and want to sell my share and start a garage specializing in certain makes of cars. What do you think?"

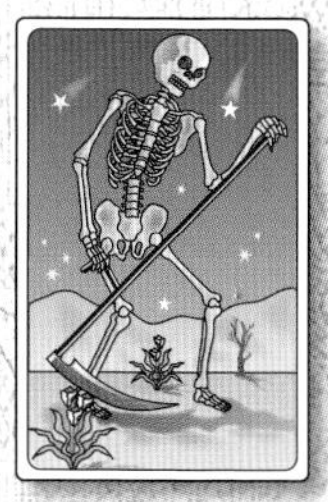

Q3 "My firm closed about six months ago. I've applied for lots of jobs at other companies, but without success. My age seems to be the problem. What can I do?"

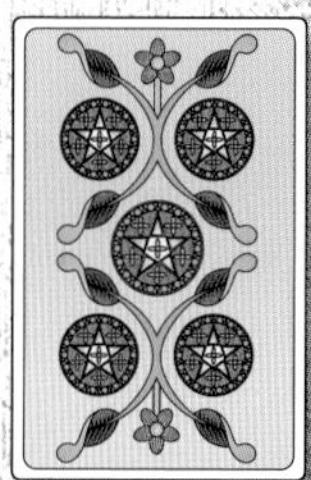

Q4 "I left my native country as a refugee after my family was killed during a civil war. I'm a qualified physiotherapist, but I need to take an examination in order to practice my profession in this country. I am worried about language problems. Will I pass?"

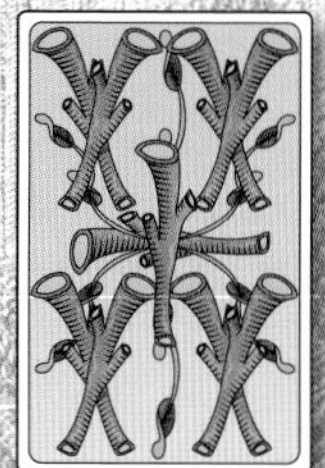

Q5 "I have written a musical play that my agent thinks may be a great success. She has sent it to well-known producer. Do you think it will be accepted?"

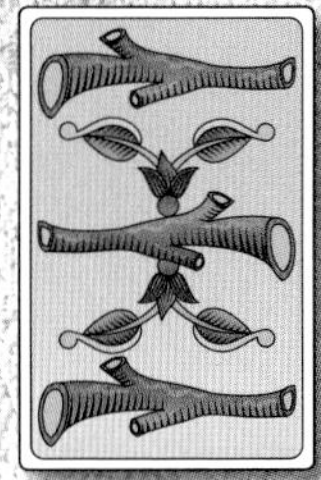
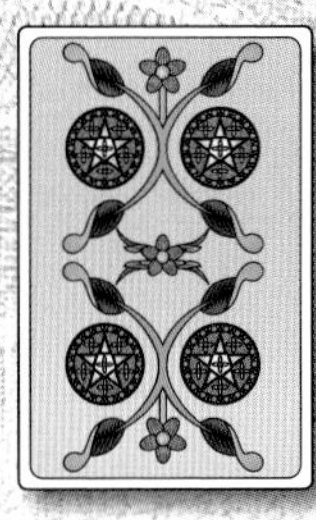

Q6 "I abandoned my university studies to work as a stockbroker. I earned lots of money and enjoyed it at first, but now I want to renew my studies to become a teacher. Will I succeed?"

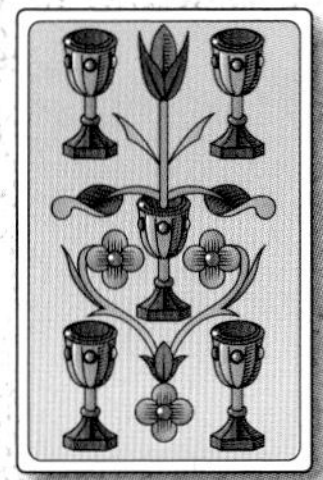

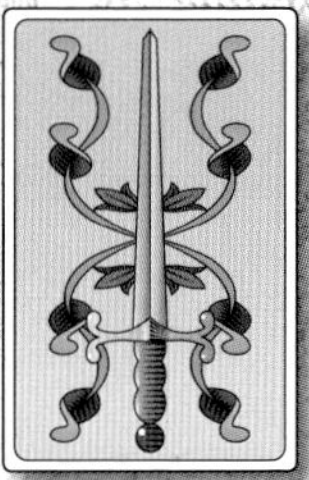

Q7 "I passed my law exams but didn't get very good grades, and I've been working as a waiter because I couldn't find work in the legal professions. Will I ever be able to find a good job as a lawyer?"

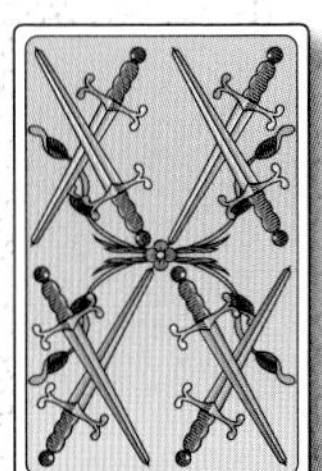

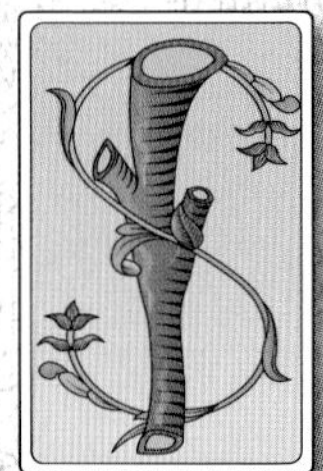

Q8 "I want to go to performing arts school to study dance and drama. I'm not beautiful, but my high school teacher said I was a natural performer. I am auditioning next week. Will they take me?"

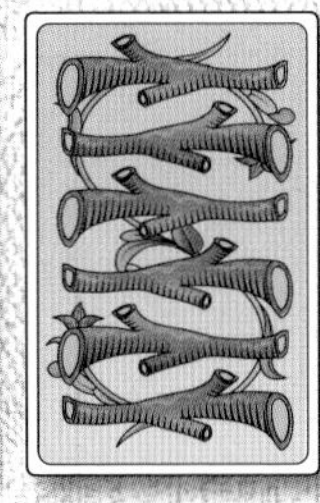

Q9 "I have started my own business, but with economic conditions being so bad at the moment, I am worried that it will collapse. Will it?"

Q10 "I've just got my degree and want to become a journalist. I've applied to four newspapers. Will I succeed?"

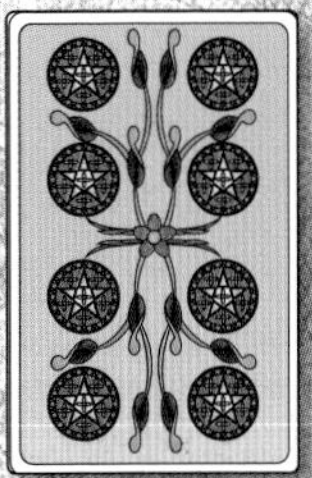
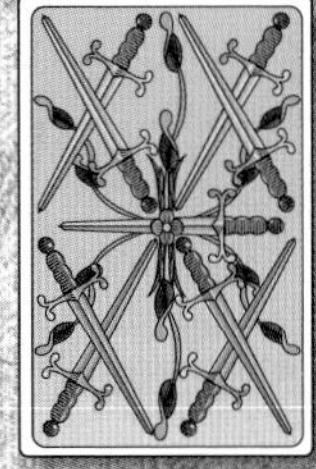

Career and Success Answers

A1 The Ten of Swords in the past represents the lowest ebb in human and national affairs, but it also brings self-honesty so that one sees things as they really are. Judgment in the present signifies a mental awakening, the end of one life and the beginning of another, change and pride in achievements, as well as a reward for past efforts. The Six of Swords in the future symbolizes risk bringing rewards, and also means success after anxiety and the end of a difficult time. More importantly for this reading, however, it indicates that traveling to a better environment will bring success.

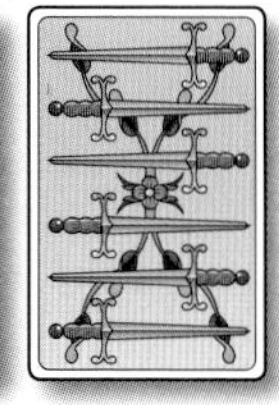

A2 Death is not always a pleasant card because it means the end of something or the sudden overturning of a way of life. However, it is also a highly spiritual card and symbolizes change, transformation, and destruction that leads to a new life. It can denote a creative or artistic struggle that ends in triumph, or the end of a difficult period in life. The Magician in the present indicates new beginnings, new opportunities, willpower, and turning thought into action. It also carries a warning of guile and trickery.

However, when positioned next to Death, the two cards cancel each other out; when they are opposite each other in a spread, they denote that there will be a delay. Since the Romany Draw only has three cards, this may not be significant. However, it could indicate that the querent will have a new beginning, but there could be a delay or deception over money and his first plan will be abandoned. The Three of Pentacles in the future paints a rosy picture of hard work, training, and consistent effort that will bring success and recognition. This could indicate that the querent's skill in his trade will result in a successful expansion in business and lead to financial rewards. When badly aspected, it does contain a warning of loss of direction, but not in this instance since Death and the Magician have canceled each other's more negative meanings. It is therefore clear that the querent's old business will end and that, being a hard worker, he will succeed in a new venture in the future. This could well be the new garage he proposes, but there is a chance it could be something else.

The Three of Wands signifies that the querent has great artistic and creative abilities. It also indicates that inspirational endeavors will be successful.

A3 Although the Tower in the past means a sudden upheaval or catastrophe and can dominate a spread, particularly if the problem is emotional, it can also represent a change of life pattern that brings eventual happiness. The Five of Pentacles in the present symbolizes the loss of work and friends, and sometimes the loss of a home, all of which can cause spiritual loneliness. However, it also carries the message that lasting friendships are made with people in similar circumstances. Happily, the future contains the Ace of Pentacles, which represents stoicism, endurance, and pride in the ability to succeed as well as a new enterprise that brings prosperity. The querent should therefore be advised to embark on a new training program, which will ensure success and happiness in the future, both in terms of career and friendships formed along the way.

A4 Death in the past represents the death of the querent's old life and the end of a troublesome period. It also symbolizes a creative or artistic struggle that leads to triumph and transformation. The King of Wands in the present could refer to a wise and generous man, a leader in his field who will give both sympathetic help and advice to the querent. The Ten of Wands in the future denotes problems that will soon be solved and burdens lifted. This will only be achieved through hard work but the results will be well worthwhile. The querent should therefore be encouraged to seek advice from someone of high authority in her field. If she does, she will receive the help she needs in her studies and will succeed and gain new business contracts.

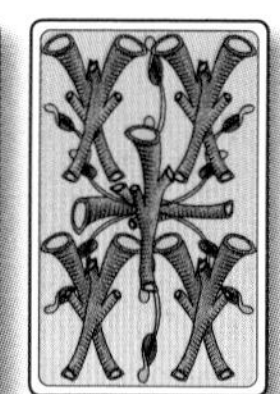

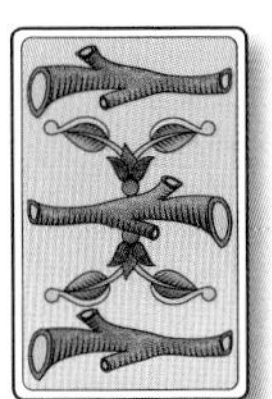

A5 The Three of Wands in the past is the card of the artist or inventor. It signifies that original or inspirational endeavors will bring recognition and success, and that artistic and creative ideas will become reality. It also indicates that the querent will receive help from a powerful associate. The Four of Pentacles in the present is another beneficial card regarding financial stability and gain, although there is a warning that care must be taken over all matters concerning money in order to avoid problems arising in the future. This could mean that the querent needs to ensure that contracts are examined carefully by a lawyer before signing them. The World in the future is the wish card of the tarot. It symbolizes material reward, success, dreams coming true, and long-distance travel over water, which could mean the musical will be a success abroad as well as at home.

A6 The Five of Cups in the past denotes a crossroads in life and new paths about to be explored. It also contains a warning that one's spiritual needs must never be ignored. It is therefore safe to assume that the querent, dissatisfied with his previous life, now wishes to help society by becoming a teacher. Strength in the present is the strongest card in the deck and signifies that the querent has integrity, inner spiritual strength, and will possibly get an offer of financial help or a scholarship. This shows that the querent obviously possesses all the qualities required to become a good teacher. The Ace of Swords in the future is the card of divine justice. It can mean changes in perspective, strength in adversity, and triumph over obstacles. The cards therefore reveal the querent may have needed to explore a different career path in the past, but must now follow his heart and retrain in this new profession. The querent's new perspective on life will indeed bring success in teaching.

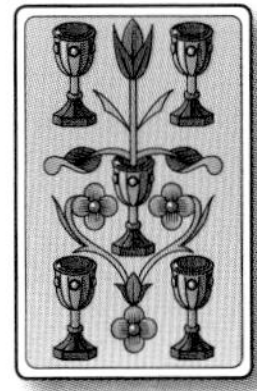

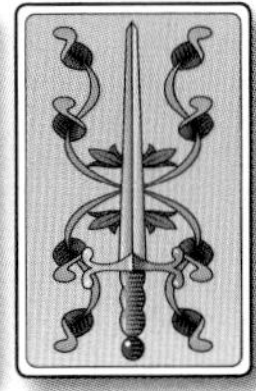

A7 The Eight of Swords can represent negativity and lack of confidence causing indecision. It probably indicates that the querent needs to develop self-honesty about his previous work ethic and where his talents truly lie. However, the card also has positive connotations, implying that restrictions will soon be lifted. The Devil in the present is a powerful and largely negative card. It signifies insensitivity through a materialistic nature dominated by physical appetites. However, it also represents an inevitable event that is good or bad, depending on the surrounding cards. Luckily, the Ace of Wands in the future is a fortunate card. It means new attitudes and a new beginning built on solid foundations that bring success and renewed confidence. So, after the querent has learned his lesson and realizes that he must be more diligent in the future, he will achieve a successful new beginning in life and work.

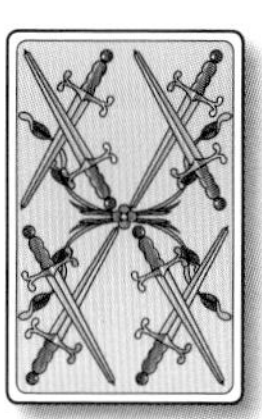

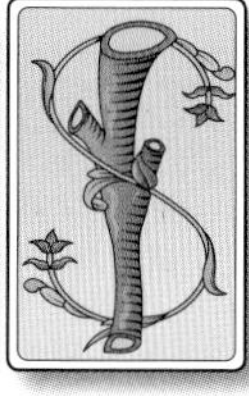

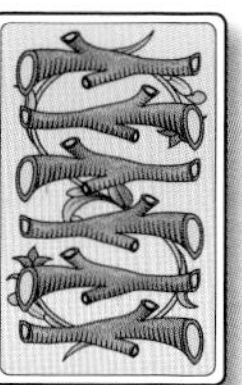

A8 The Knave of Wands in the past represents an adaptable and spiritual young person of either sex who is under 21, with creative potential, and looking for a direction in life. It can denote a messenger bringing either news from a loved one or a pleasant surprise concerning money. Although it sometimes shows fear of domination, it also symbolizes creative inspiration or talent that needs to be developed. The Six of Wands in the present is the career card of the Minor Arcana. It signifies triumph in career, success after struggle, victory in a difficult situation, wonderful news, the fulfillment of ambitions, solutions to a major problem, diplomacy overcoming opposition, and public acclaim and satisfaction. It is therefore safe to conclude that the result of the querent's audition will be positive and bring her a great deal of joy and success. The Hierophant in the future denotes a desire for social approval, a love of convention, established religion, teaching, spirituality, self-honesty, hidden secrets revealed, and more importantly, inspirational genius in the performing arts. So the querent's future will certainly be successful in her chosen field. At some point she could also decide to teach her skills to others.

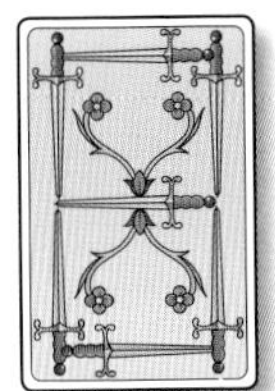

A9 The Seven of Swords in the past indicates that frugality, careful thought, foresight, and diplomatic relations with suppliers are needed to achieve success. It also warns against procrastination because this could have negative consequences for the future if the querent fails to deal with problems as they arise. The Two of Cups in the present can mean that a friend will help, but probably in a limited capacity, and also that a contract or agreement will be signed. The Seven of Pentacles in the future signifies that consistent work is needed to achieve a successful result. It can also reveal that a loan will take longer than expected to be granted. So the conclusion is that, although there are positive cards in the spread that indicate the querent will receive help from a friend and a contract will be offered, the querent must also make immediate, positive, and determined efforts if success is to be achieved.

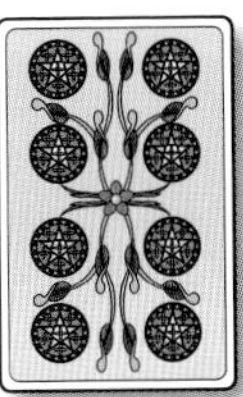

A10 The Eight of Pentacles in the past expresses the combination of talent and energy. It indicates that the skills and talents of the querent can develop in a profession that brings success and money. However, the Nine of Swords in the present can mean sad news, loss, or despair. It also denotes a difficult choice entailing sacrifice. This could indicate that the querent will receive an offer of a job but that it will not be as prestigious as originally hoped for, or that the querent will consider the offer belittling and could refuse. The Hermit in the future signifies delayed achievement and caution when choosing an unfamiliar but necessary path. However, its strongest meaning is that wise counsel will bring inner enlightenment. The querent should therefore listen carefully to advice given by someone more experienced and act upon it. If she does this, success will eventually be achieved.

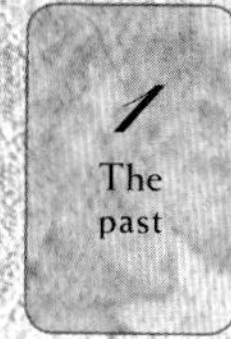

HEALTH AND WELL-BEING QUESTIONS

Refer to page 20-21 for instructions on how to perform the Romany Draw; see pages 108-115 for the answers to these questions.

Q1 "Last year I nursed my mother until she died, lost my brother through a heart attack, and now my husband is very ill. I'm trying to be strong but my nerves are so bad I feel I might collapse at any moment. Will things get better?"

Q2 "The man I was living with has gone back to his wife and children. I've had to move out of our apartment since I can't afford it on my own and I feel tired, run down, and depressed. Why should this happen to me?"

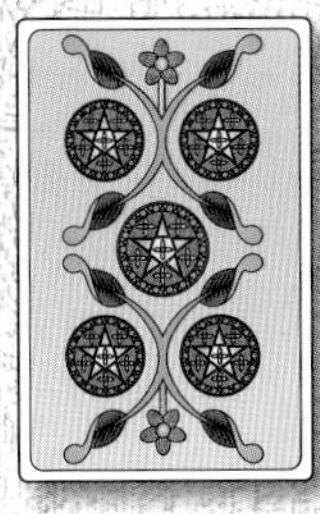
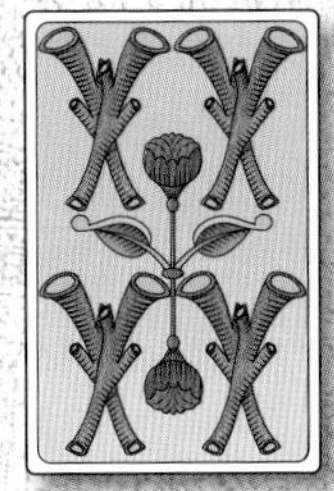

Q3 "My husband is in the army and is often away from home. We have two young children and live with his mother, who has cataracts in her eyes but won't have surgery. Yesterday she was nearly hit by a car. What is going to happen to her?"

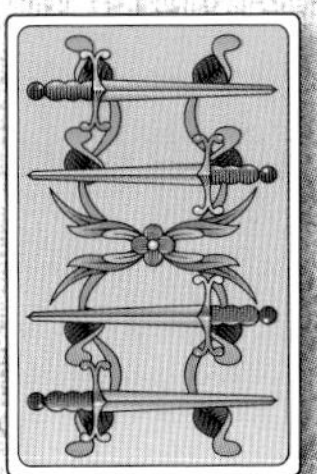

Q4 "My son used to work every hour of the day, but when his wife got cancer, he closed his business and nursed her until she died. He's studying naturopathy now. Will he be successful?"

Q5 "A specialist examined me and found that I have a growth in the bowel. He seemed worried and said I'll have to undergo surgery. Do you think everything will be okay?"

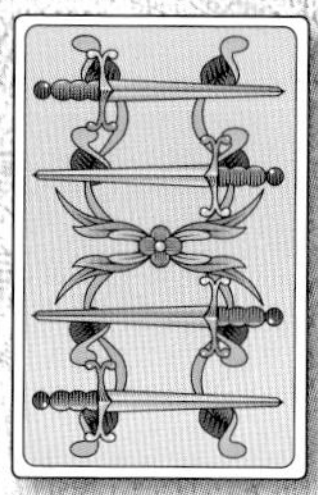

Q6 "After my third miscarriage, my doctor told me I probably wouldn't be able to carry a child full term. My husband and I would like to adopt, but the process is so strict, I think I will want to die if they refuse. What will happen?"

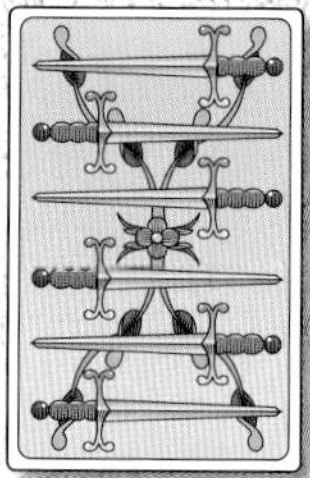

Q7 "I have trained for years as a swimmer, but two weeks ago I fell down some stairs, broke two ribs, and fractured a shoulder. I feel I'm finished as an athlete. Am I right?"

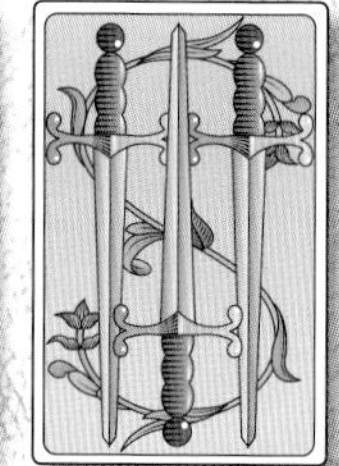

Q8 "My husband has a back injury and he cannot work. He has been advised to undergo a new kind of surgery that could be risky. Should he go ahead?"

Q9 "I worked hard to build up my travel business, but when I retired due to ill health, my lover said I no longer have anything to offer and left me. I feel old and useless. Will things ever get better?"

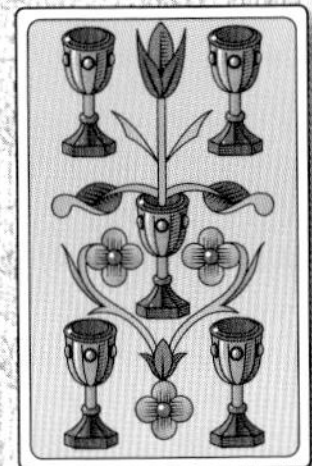

Q10 "I was in an automobile accident. My wife died and I was in the hospital for months as a result. I've now been awarded compensation. What lies ahead for me?"

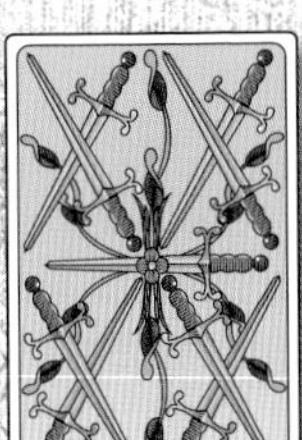
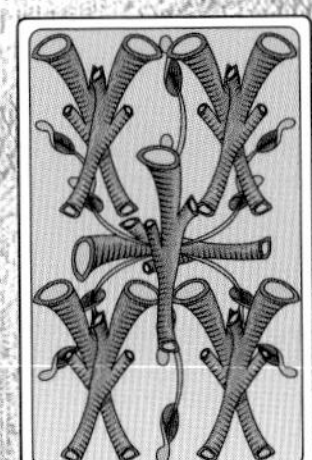

HEALTH AND WELL-BEING ANSWERS

A1 The Moon in the past symbolizes the subconscious, dreams, illusion, imagination, creativity, mystery, hidden forces, deception, and fluctuation. More importantly here, it denotes a loved one's misfortune, uncertainty, an emotional crisis, and storms weathered, illustrating the suffering and the strength of the querent. The Three of Cups in the present represents the feminine element that brings emotional growth, love, and happiness in all relationships. It also signifies sensitivity to others and a great capacity for giving that brings love and friendship. The High Priestess makes the future a happy one, because not only does it mean that the querent loves to learn, could have creative ability, psychic power, and esoteric knowledge, but also that she is protected spiritually.

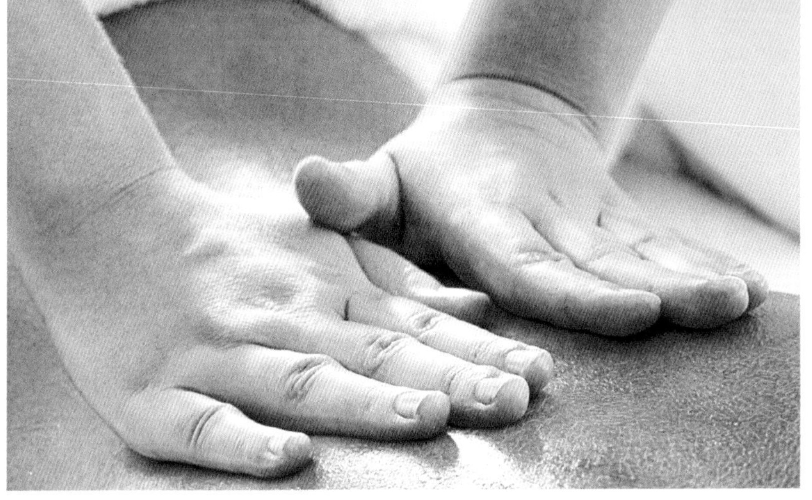

The Four of Swords means illness and hospitalization. When accompanied by the Star, there will be a positive recovery, both spiritually and physically.

A2 The Tower in the past is no surprise, denoting a sudden unexpected shock or catastrophe. It also means illusions shattered and the closing of the karmic circle, selfish ambitions destroyed, a disruption of life that will be better in the long term, and sometimes a flash of inspiration that brings the beginning of enlightenment. The Five of Pentacles in the present indicates a mind that is overruled by emotion, bringing loss of judgment, disappointment, sorrow, loss of work or position, loss of lover, loss of home, enforced restrictions, and physical and spiritual loneliness. There is also the meaning that real friendships could be made with those in the same circumstances, and when next to positive cards, it can also indicate both a new start and faith regained in oneself. This could certainly be possible with the Eight of Wands in the future, as it means the end of a quiet period or delay, sudden changes that bring progress, overseas connections, and a good time to try something new. It is symbolic of movement, speed, haste, unexpected news, a trip by air, and the sudden arrows of love. So it seems that after some emotional suffering, the querent will recognize her faults and learn to give more than take, value others for character rather than money or status, could visit friends in another place, and could meet real love unexpectedly.

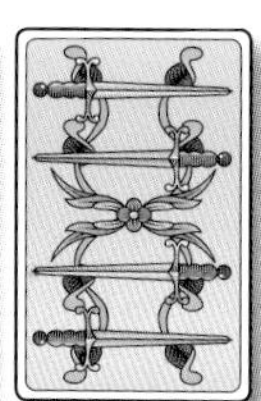

and at his best in a difficult situation. It can also indicate that a conflict needs to be faced. When near cards denoting illness, such as the Four of Swords, it represents a surgeon. So the cards reveal that, after the shock of the previous day, the older woman may decide to have the operation. She may also seek legal redress for the accident.

A3 The Wheel of Fortune represents the gaining of balance and wisdom through evolution, the capriciousness of fate, and a sudden change, mostly for the better but sometimes creating problems. These could be the result of past efforts and will eventually prove beneficial. All these meanings could apply to the trauma the querent's mother-in-law suffered the day before and its effect on her thinking. The Four of Swords in the present symbolizes peace and order coming after struggle or chaos, administration in legal matters, a voluntary retreat after a testing time in order to think matters through, and importantly, hospitalization and convalescence. If badly aspected, it represents a feeling of isolation, postponing a decision, and the need to be tactful, and although the Knight of Swords is not a negative card, those feelings could have affected the querent or her mother-in-law after the near-accident. The Knight of Swords denotes a courageous man under 35, who could be foreign, is a passionate fighter, skilled in defense,

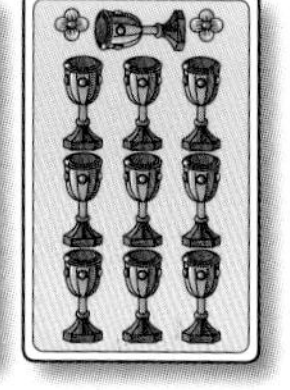

A4 The Hanged Man in the past symbolizes a willing sacrifice that entails suffering and loss or hardship, but that will transform a life. It also symbolizes forgiveness that brings inner peace and wisdom, which probably indicates that the man's grief and anger at his wife's death have been transformed. Another meaning is that a decision will bring peace and the reversal of a way of life. In the present, the Two of Pentacles, positively aspected next to the Ten of Cups, signifies literary ability and a journey to a new home or country. It also indicates skillful manipulation and harmony during sudden domestic or financial changes, new moves to make, success in one direction, and most importantly here, that the use of one talent will bring reward. It is no surprise then to find the future holding the Ten of Cups, bringing deep and lasting spiritual happiness, fame, prestige, publicity, honor, secure success in a public sphere, the love of friends, and a journey that has a happy ending. Since the Two of Pentacles means a journey to a new home or country and the Ten of Cups represents buying, selling, and successful legal matters pertaining to property and residence, the querent's son will be successful, move to a new place, and could possibly meet someone he could love and marry.

The Six of Swords indicates the end of a stressful period and some good news that will lead to happiness and fulfillment.

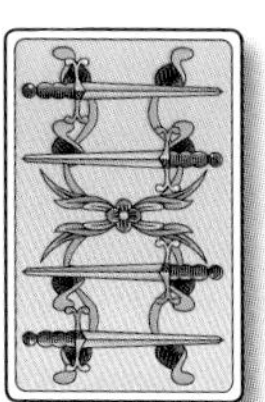

A5 The King of Cups in the past represents a professional man over 35, worldly, powerful, and who could be connected with medicine. Sometimes he can be crafty and put himself first, but he can also be sensitive, creative, kind, and warm-hearted. He tends to hide his emotions but gives reliable advice and help. The Four of Swords in the present means administration in legal matters, both civic and personal, a voluntary retreat after a testing time to think things through, and peace and order coming after struggle or chaos. It also indicates hospitalization and convalescence. If badly aspected, it can signify a decision postponed, a need for diplomacy, or feelings of isolation, but with the Star in the future there can be no negative meanings in this spread. The Star symbolizes refreshing the mind and spirit after a period of darkness, spiritual strength and guidance, rebirth, optimism, good friends, love of others, and unselfish help given. So the outlook for the querent is good and he may also use his convalescence to finish something creative.

A6 The Moon can denote hidden forces, mystery, dreams, illusion, imagination, the occult, intuition, and deception. So with this card in the past, it is possible the querent feels she is being punished for something. On a practical level, however, it denotes a loved one's misfortune, which could mean the baby, an emotional crisis and uncertainty, but also storms weathered. The loss will not affect her for long, because the Hermit in the present symbolizes being guided by one's own inner light and being protected by spiritual strength. It also denotes caution when choosing an unfamiliar but necessary path, an enlightened journey, wise counsel, sudden insight solving problems, and a delayed achievement. The Six of Swords in the future shows that her worries will end, for as well as indicating flight or travel to a better environment and risk bringing reward, it also denotes the end of a difficult time, obstacles removed, and success after a period of stress or anxiety.

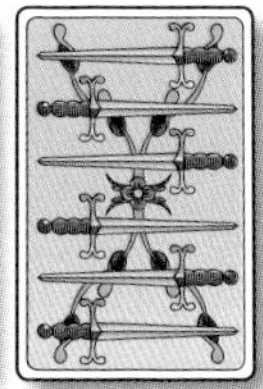

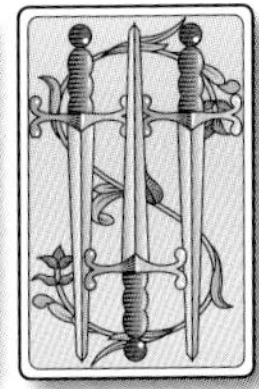

A7 The Devil in the past implies negative power used selfishly or unwisely, through ignorance, fear, greed, superstition, the dominance of physical appetites, material gain, and insensitivity. It also denotes a sudden event or change, which must refer to the accident. Although the Devil is a negative card that can dominate the others in a spread, the positive Chariot in the future is equally powerful and negates the Devil's influence. The Three of Swords in the present can signify permanent or temporary separation, disruption, a marriage or partnership broken, upheaval, and pain followed by healing. There is also a sense that the ground is clearing for something new. As it is positively aspected next to the Chariot, the Three of Swords' other meaning of dwelling on old hurts cannot apply, because the Chariot brings patience, endurance, triumph over difficulties, success, sudden news, fast travel, and prestige and wealth through sustained effort. So the querent's strength, endurance, and patience will help her triumph over her difficulties.

The Five of Cups indicates that the querent is about to embark on a journey and take a new path in life. The card also warns that spiritual needs must never be ignored if the querent is to achieve happiness.

A8 Although the Moon can mean uncertainty, hidden forces, and deception, it can also signify an emotional crisis, a loved one's misfortune, and storms weathered. The Knight of Swords can represent a conflict to be faced, and more importantly when next to cards denoting illness, a surgeon. The Magician, symbolizing willpower turning thought into action, is a happy symbol for the future when in context with the other two cards because it means that the right decision will be made and there will be a new life and successful employment for the querent's husband.

A9 The Five of Cups in the past is symbolic of one thing ending and something new beginning, an inheritance, new paths to explore, or a new life to start. It also has negative meanings of a love affair ended, loss and regrets, a mistake made, and the warning never to ignore one's inner voice or spiritual needs. This illustrates not only what happened, but also that the querent may have been led astray by physical attraction or outer appearance and did not listen to his intuition. The Six of Cups in the present points to something positive that has its roots in the past, such as work or contacts bringing benefits, a long-held ambition, an old friend who will reappear, and even a love affair. It also implies that the result of past actions may influence the present, so there is a warning not to repeat previous mistakes. The future shows the wish card of the Major Arcana, for the World means lessons learned, spiritual triumph, material reward, joy, happiness, dreams coming true, and possibly a journey over water. As the Five of Cups means a new life starting, and the Six represents a love affair, the World must show that the querent has learned from his mistakes and will value the spiritual above the physical in future. He will therefore be happy in love and successful in business.

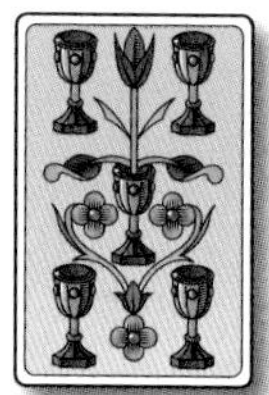

 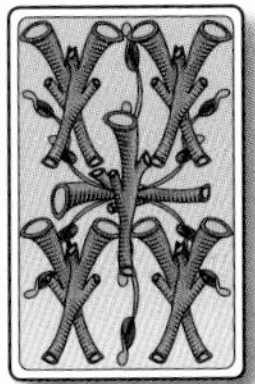 

A10 The Nine of Swords in the past means a loss, death, accident, despair, sorrow, and patient suffering borne with courage and strength. The Ten of Wands in the present signifies problems solved, burdens soon to be lifted, new ideas and business offers, and also an overseas trip. The Four of Wands, as well as denoting a gifted and successful designer or inventor, the gathering of a harvest, and close family ties, implies that there will be a peaceful period away from everyday worries. The cards therefore show that the querent will travel and be offered new and pleasing work in the future.

The Chariot symbolizes endurance, sustained effort, and triumph over difficulties if the querent can overcome negativity and learn to be patient.

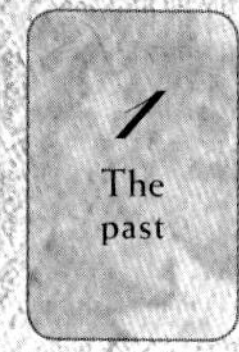

Personal Character Questions

Refer to page 20-21 for instructions on how to perform the Romany Draw; see pages 120-125 for the answers to these questions.

Q1 "I've been modeling for two years and think I have the chance to be famous and earn lots of money, but the man I love wants me to give it up when we marry. His family is wealthy and he doesn't understand what it was like for me growing up poor. Don't you think I'm right and he's being selfish?"

Q2 "My husband sold his business and went off with another woman. I only received a small divorce settlement because he lied about his assets. My lawyer wants to challenge it, but I just want to move on with my life. Am I being stupid?"

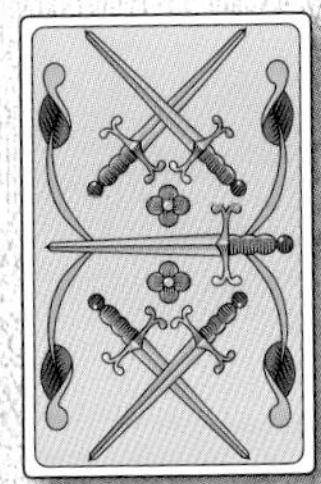

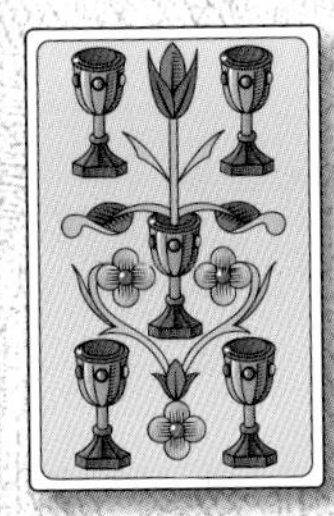

Q3 "I won a scholarship to study veterinary science. My best friend says I won't have money for years and I'm stupid to be more concerned with animals than living well and having fun. Do you think he's right?"

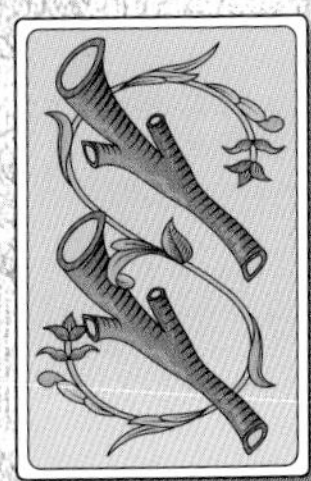

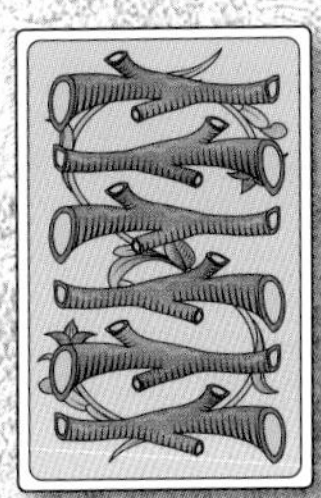

Q4 "I wrote a children's story and my husband drew the illustrations. A television company wants to film it but my husband wants me to refuse the offer. I think it's because his illustrations won't be featured. I'm going to accept. Am I right?"

Q5 "I'm a bank manager but am running for local office in the next election because I feel that I could do a good job and help people. Am I doing the right thing and will I get elected?"

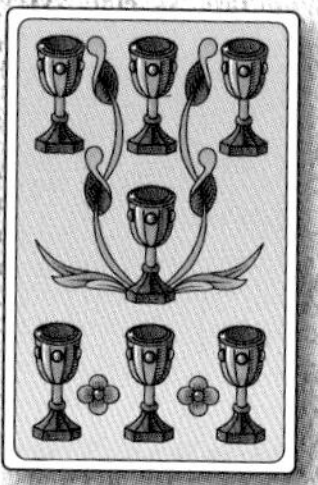

Q6 "I was caught forging credit cards and spent six months in jail. I now know that money is not as important as people are and I want to train to be a nurse. With my record, do I have a chance?"

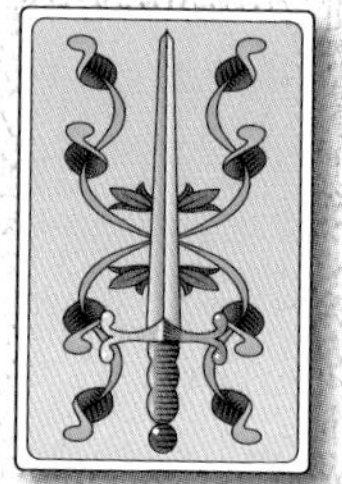
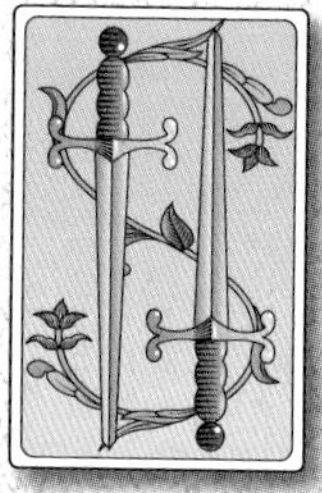

Q7 "After I failed my exams, I was devastated when my teacher told me that arrogance and laziness were the causes. I'm repeating the year's studies now. Will I pass this time and get into the university of my choice?"

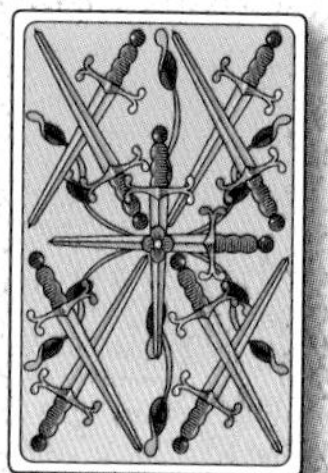

Q8 "My boyfriend told me he's in love with someone else who is a 'giver.' I'm not a taker! Why have I had to suffer?"

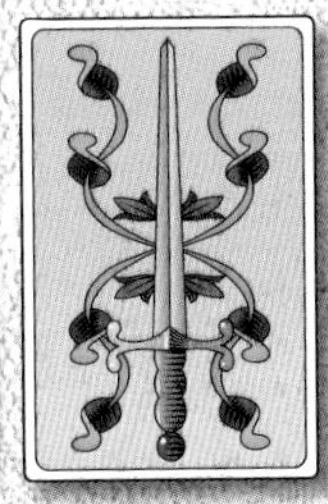

Q9 "I'm an immigrant and I drive a taxi. I'm taking night classes to improve my job prospects but I feel the others I attend school with look down on me. Will I ever get somewhere with all the studying I'm doing?"

Q10 "My husband can be loving and kind, but he became violent toward me after he lost his job. I have left him. He says he really loves me and has agreed to see a counselor if I will go back. Does he really mean it and will it help?"

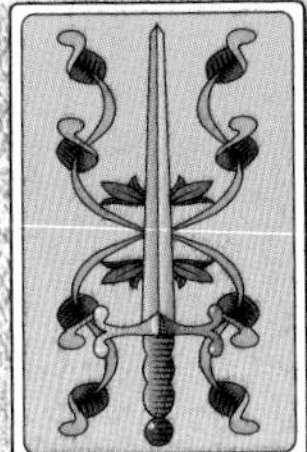

PERSONAL CHARACTER ANSWERS

A1 The Devil in the past represents a strong power used selfishly and unwisely through fear or greed, and a life dominated by physical appetite and material gain. The Knave of Pentacles in the present could symbolize the querent, who is diligent and ambitious, but when badly aspected, it describes wasted talent, intellectual snobbery, and most importantly, unrealistic ambitions and a young person who is often materialistic and mean with money. The Two of Swords in the future signifies balanced forces or a stalemate, a sense of equilibrium, help and friendship in adversity, good coming out of evil, and making a difficult choice that brings satisfaction and spiritual peace. In this case, as both cards are badly aspected by the dominant Devil, it means the querent could make the wrong choice through indecision, living in the past, or self-deception. She could be expecting too much success in her future career, may be growing fonder of money than people, and unless she learns to see herself and others honestly, she will never learn to give of herself, to love others, or be content with her life.

A2 The Five of Swords can mean that one must accept the inevitable and face defeat courageously in order to move onward and upward in a new direction. When badly aspected, as it is here next to the Hanged Man, it also implies that fear or insecure foundations may cause humiliation and defeat. However, although the Hanged Man can mean loss and hardship, it also denotes a spiritual decision that brings serenity, and an inner strength that results in a new way of life. The Five of Cups in the future symbolizes the end of one thing and the beginning of something new. The cards therefore signify that the querent should listen to her inner voice, and as long as she does not ignore her spiritual needs, she will embark on a new life that will be happier than ever before.

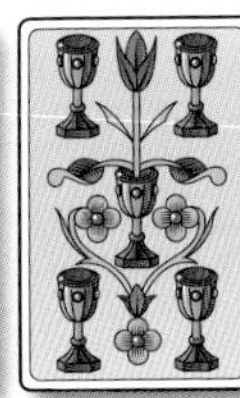

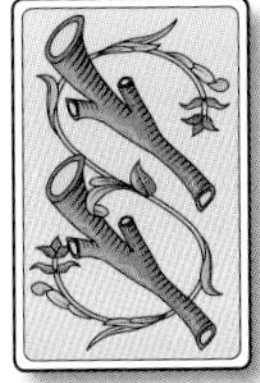

A3 The Two of Wands describes the querent's personality and attitude to life. It denotes intellectual achievement, high motives, help from people in authority, justice, tolerance, overcoming obstacles, and success won through strength and vision. It indicates that courage, willpower, and initiative have led him to achieve a maturity that will bring both future happiness and lasting success. The Hanged Man, apart from meaning a willing sacrifice or decision that causes loss or hardship, also denotes a transformation resulting in inner strength, peace, wisdom, and the reversal of a way of life. The Six of Wands is the career card of the Minor Arcana. It has the triumphant meaning of wonderful news, victory in a difficult situation, a solution to a major problem, success after struggle, diplomacy overcoming opposition, fulfillment of ambition, and success in a career that brings public acclaim and satisfaction. Together the cards show that the querent is more focused on service than money, and will be highly successful in both studies and future career. However, there is a sting in the tail, as it also means triumph soured by others' envy.

A4 The King of Cups in the past can denote the husband, who is over 35, has creative talent, and may work in the fields of education, law, medicine, or religion. He is warm-hearted and sensitive, hides his emotions, and can give good advice and help, but he can also be crafty and selfish. The Two of Cups in the present symbolizes deep understanding of another, spirituality and emotion creating a permanent bond, and a love affair or a lasting friendship. Although this shows that the querent is right to assume that her husband is jealous, happily the card also means a reconciliation after a parting, a rivalry ended, a new partnership, and a contract or agreement signed. The Seven of Cups in the future signifies that there will be a happy solution. It denotes an unexpected and exceptional offer that requires wisdom, mental ability, and creative inspiration to ensure the right choice, and this will bring surprising rewards and a dream fulfilled for the artist and writer.

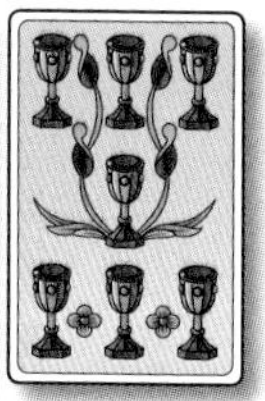

A5 The Ace of Pentacles indicates that the querent has had a comfortable, even wealthy, existence because it means materialism, love of possessions, pride in the ability to succeed, gold, luxury, sensuousness, gifts, legacies, prosperity, security built on a firm foundation, and an enterprise commencing that brings solid financial benefit. If badly aspected, it can mean greed and overconfidence, but here it is next to the Emperor, representing worldly authority, wealth, power, intellect, passion, romance, self-discipline, creative and mental activity, knowledge through experience, and a governing body or force. The outcome therefore looks promising. The Seven of Cups can symbolize an unexpected and exceptional offer, the realization of a dream, and creative inspiration and mental ability bringing surprising rewards. Pentacles and Cups together can signify care for others, healing, or drama, and when combined with the Emperor can indicate a career in politics.

A6 Although the Ace of Swords in the past is the symbol of divine justice, it also represents a strong force for good or evil and an inevitable event that changes the querent's perspective on life. The Two of Swords in the present signifies a wrong choice through self-deception and living in the past. However, Judgment is a strongly positive card and means a sense of equilibrium, help in adversity, good coming out of evil, and a difficult choice that brings spiritual peace and satisfaction to the querent. The cards therefore imply that the querent will undergo a spiritual reincarnation and experience a new lease on life, release, change, renewal, the end of one period and the beginning of another, justified pride in achievement, and a mental awakening that brings success.

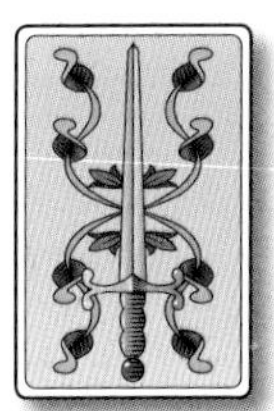
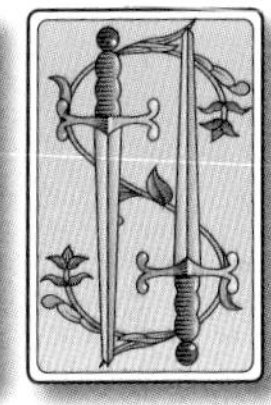

A7 The Ten of Swords in the past means the lowest point in both human and national affairs as well as self-honesty. When favorably aspected, as it is here with the Seven of Pentacles in the present, it signifies the end of spiritual darkness, rebirth, and self-acceptance. The Seven of Pentacles can be interpreted as "procrastination is the thief of time." The querent must therefore avoid laziness and work consistently to achieve a successful conclusion. Its most positive meaning is that things are changing and that recent efforts are about to bear fruit. It could also indicate that a scholarship or money will be awarded but could be a little late. With the Magician in the future, symbolizing a new beginning, the querent will learn new skills and develop his talents in a new life. However, with the Magician's darker meaning of guile and trickery, along with the Ten of Swords in the past, there is also a warning that the querent must work hard to fight conceit and laziness in the future.

A8 The Devil indicates a strong negative power used selfishly or unwisely, caused by greed, fear, ignorance, or superstition. It also symbolizes a life dominated by physical appetites and material gain, as well as a lack of sensitivity. It can signify a sudden, inexorable event that, depending on the cards near it, may be either positive or negative. The Ace of Swords, which means "you reap what you sow," indicates that this event will completely change the querent's perspective on life. It is clear that she has lessons to learn. The Ace can mean strength in adversity, and when near the Devil, disappointment followed by victory. The victory comes with the Knight of Wands, a man who has traveled and who the querent will meet when she moves to another place and starts a new life.

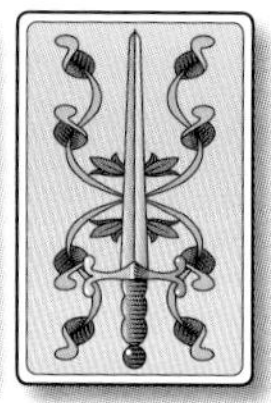

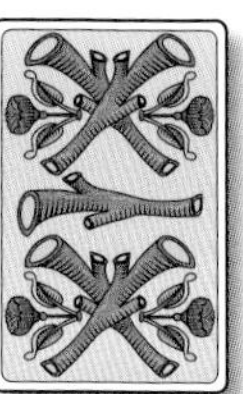

A9 The Queen of Swords in the past can represent a struggle between spiritual and material values, sadness, and privation. It can also symbolize a woman who is strong, cautious, self-reliant, and intelligent, or a woman who is intolerant, spiteful, and a good friend or a bad enemy. The Queen often denotes a strong-minded mother, who may have children who are timid and lacking self-confidence. The Five of Wands in the present is a positive card, and in this context it means that a determined struggle will overcome material adversity, but warns that mental ability is needed to triumph and bring a change for the better. However, it also implies that unfulfilled desires could bring bitterness. So the querent must continue his studies, particularly as the future card is the High Priestess, who represents mystery, esoteric knowledge, philosophy, and spiritual protection. She is one of the strongest and most positive cards in the deck, and indicates that love of learning and creative talents will bring cultural advancement.

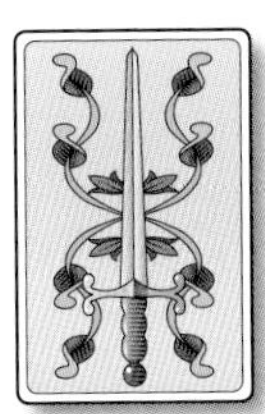
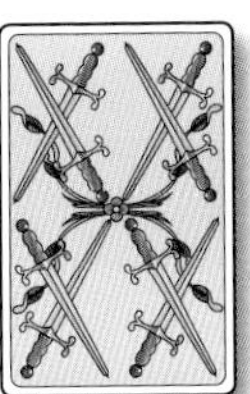

A10 The Ace of Swords in the past represents something inevitable that will change the querent's perspective on life, strength in adversity, and triumph over obstacles. Here, it is badly aspected next to the Eight of Swords, so it also denotes disappointment preceding triumph. However, although the Eight of Swords means that self-honesty, confidence, and attention to detail are needed to change things, it also signifies that restrictions will soon be lifted and bonds broken. That could mainly apply to the querent's husband, but because it is positively aspected next to the Eight of Cups, it also represents hurts healed, progress made, and a new self-confidence. The Eight of Cups denotes a new maturity and a deep spiritual change brought about by disillusionment and suffering. It also means forgetting the past, seeking new activities, leaving a situation or place behind, and meeting artistic and spiritual people who become genuine friends. So the verdict is to stay away—both the querent's and her husband's future will be changed for the better if they move on separately.

The Eight of Cups encourages the querent to leave past problems and negative influences behind, and walk into the future with an open heart, ready to welcome new and genuine friendships.

Full Reading

This is an example of a full reading using the Romany Draw (see page 20-21 for instructions). Although this spread is generally used to answer a specific question, here it is interpreted in terms of all aspects of the querent's life, including love, career, health, and character.

1: The Past

The Nine of Swords in the past reveals that the querent has been going through a negative period. This could have entailed illness, loss of a relative, lover, or friend, loss of a business, making a difficult choice that brought about sacrifice, a feeling of isolation, a sense of despair, and even self-punishment. However, it also indicates that the querent suffered these difficulties with patience, strength, and courage. In addition, when the Nine of Swords is positively aspected, as it is here by the Chariot and Strength, it signifies that the past is over and an active and rewarding new existence is about to begin. It also means that time is a healer.

2: The Present

The Chariot is a positive card, symbolizing the balance of positive and negative forces in order to achieve triumph and success in life. It can signify that sustained effort, patience, endurance, and a victory over stress and problems will eventually bring success, wealth, and prestige for the querent. It can also mean sudden news and fast travel.

3: The Future

Strength has no negative meanings and is the strongest card in the tarot, being both spiritual and practical. Finding this card in a spread reveals that the querent has both mental and spiritual strength. It can represent the spiritual overcoming the material, power and courage used wisely, and love conquering hate. On a more practical level, it predicts a once-in-a-lifetime offer that the querent should accept. Also, when Strength comes after the Chariot, it indicates that the querent will show great strength when facing future trials.

Interpretation

The querent has come through a sad, troubled, and trying time with spiritual strength. He or she is now looking forward to a future that, although it will require consistent effort, patience, and endurance, will also bring success and wealth. This will be helped by a sudden offer that could entail a journey and that will ensure lasting success and happiness.

The Nine of Swords signifies a time of trouble for the querent, but when combined with the positive Chariot and Strength, those problem are obviously in the past and the querent is ready to look forward to a future filled with enduring happiness.

The Celtic Cross

The Celtic Cross is one of the most popular spreads in use today and is generally used to foretell future prospects. It has ten positions and is therefore one of the more complicated tarot spreads that you can use. Combinations of cards in various positions in the spread are looked at, concentrating first on the Major Arcana and then including the influence of the Minor Arcana. The full reading at the end of the chapter shows how to incorporate the meanings of all ten cards into a single interpretation.

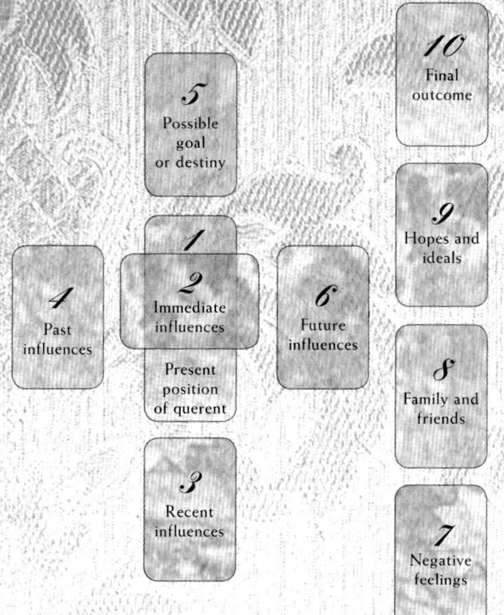

MAJOR ARCANA: INFLUENCES QUESTIONS

These questions look at combinations of Major Arcana cards and concentrate on positions one to six, signifying the querent's past, present, and future influences. Refer to page 22-23 for instructions on how to perform the Celtic Cross; see pages 136-139 for the answers to these questions.

Q1 The Magician appears in position one, representing the present position of the querent, and the Devil in position two, symbolizing the immediate influences on the querent. How would you interpret these cards?

Q2 What kind of influences are affecting the querent if the Empress is in position two, the area of immediate influences, and the Chariot in position three, the area of recent influences?

Q3 What kind of immediate and recent influences do the Lovers in position two and Death in position three denote?

Q4 What significance do the High Priestess in position two and the Moon in position four have with regard to the querent's immediate and past influences?

Q5 How would you interpret the Hanged Man in position three, recent influences, and the Emperor in position four, past influences?

Q6 Assess the recent and past influences operating on the querent if the Tower appears in position three and the Hermit in position four. What interpretation would you give?

Q7 If Strength lies in position three and Justice in position four, what recent and past influences are affecting the querent's actions and attitudes?

Q8 If Death in position four represents past influences, how does this affect the Moon in position five, symbolizing the querent's possible goal or destiny?

Q9 In position four is the High Priestess and in position five the Hanged Man. What is your interpretation of the querent's past influences and their effect on his or her possible goal or destiny?

Q10 The Wheel of Fortune in position five represents the querent's possible goal or destiny. The Hermit in position six denotes future influences. How would you interpret this pair of cards?

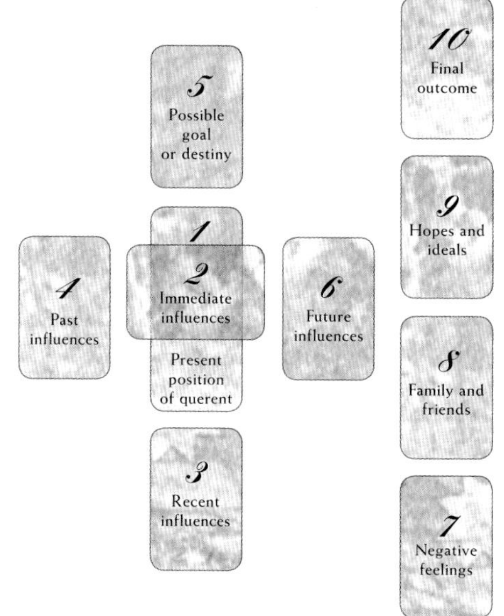

Major Arcana: Influences Answers

A1 The Magician in position one describes the querent, who is intellectually and creatively gifted, has a positive attitude, and is an excellent communicator. It also symbolizes starting a new career or new beginnings. The Devil in position two, immediate influences, indicates a sudden unexpected event that will change the querent's life, for good or ill, depending on the other cards in the spread. When next to the Magician, it can also mean a delay. So, if there are positive cards in most of the other positions, the querent may achieve future professional success but only after a lesson has been learned.

A2 The Empress in position two, immediate influences, indicates that a natural course of events will occur that require strength and patience. When the Empress is followed by the Chariot, it also means an important financial increase. The Chariot in position three, recent influences, predicts strength and victory, but also warns against manipulation from others.

A3 The Lovers in position two, immediate influences, indicates that the querent must make a difficult choice that will test values and demand total honesty. When Death comes after the Lovers, it means the end of a marriage or romance. In position three, recent influences, Death reveals that a way of life has finished or is about to end. This has led to a more positive and tolerant outlook that will bring happiness.

A4 The High Priestess in position two, immediate influences, shows that the querent possesses unused creative or artistic talent or unrecognized psychic sense that a generous and caring person will help the querent to develop. The Moon in position four, past influences, reveals that the querent has lately experienced a time of uncertainty and insecurity, but this helped the querent to realize what he or she really wanted from life.

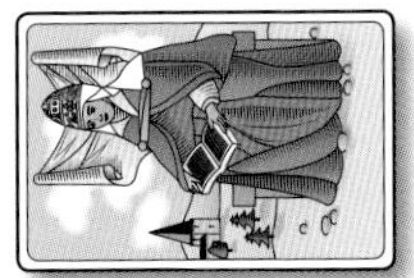

A5 When in position three, recent influences, the Hanged Man means that a sacrifice has already been made or is about to happen that will bring peace and inner strength. The Emperor in position four, past influences, indicates that an older person or an established source has guided the querent wisely.

A6 In position three, recent influences, the Tower signifies that the querent's life will be easier if he or she can learn to accept changes. In position four, past influences, the Hermit indicates that the querent has had to clear away all negative influences before finding a new road that leads to the true destination.

A7 Strength has no negative meanings. It symbolizes courage and an offer of a lifetime that must be taken. In position three, recent influences, it reveals that past trials that have been courageously endured have brought inner strength, courage, integrity, and a balanced nature. Justice, another positive card, can denote a well-balanced personality and mind, integrity, and honesty.
In position four, past influences, it shows that the querent has struggled to bring order out of chaos, has used self-discipline to organize daily life and eradicate mental confusion, and finally learned to recognize and acknowledge personal failings.

A8 In position four, past influences, Death means the querent has had to accept that things and people change as they develop and mature. The Moon in position five, possible goal or destiny, reveals that if the querent can face facts honestly, peace and stability will be achieved.

A9 The High Priestess in position four, past influences, shows that the querent's self-confidence has been weakened by disloyal friends. The Hanged Man in position five, possible goal or destiny, denotes a new serenity through finding spiritual strength.

A10 The Wheel of Fortune in position five, possible goal or destiny, indicates that the querent should examine all new opportunities thoroughly before refusing. When in position six, future influences, the Hermit tells the querent to trust intuition.

The Hermit in position six, future influences, reveals that a flash of insight will guide the querent into making the right decision.

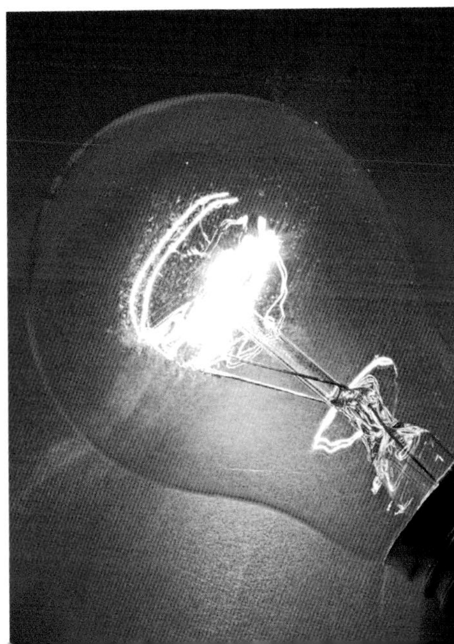

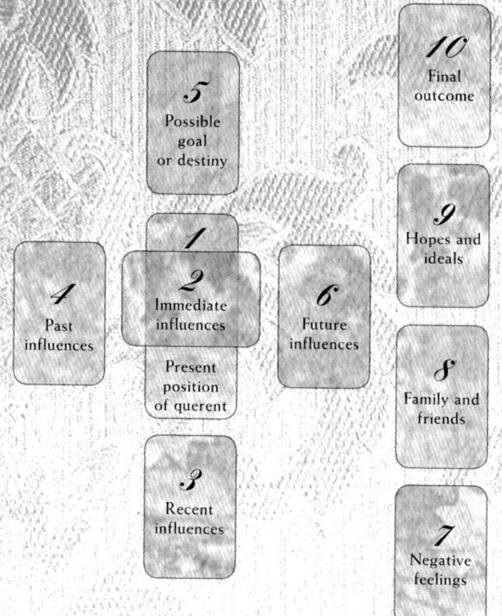

MAJOR ARCANA: FEELINGS QUESTIONS

These questions look at combinations of Major Arcana cards and concentrate on positions seven to nine, signifying the querent's positive and negative feelings and the effect of family and friends. Refer to page 22-23 for instructions on how to perform the Celtic Cross; see pages 144-148 for the answers to these questions.

Q1 How would Judgment in position five, symbolizing the querent's possible goal or destiny, and the World in position eight, representing family and friends, affect each other?

Q2 If the Chariot appears in position five and the Star in position nine, how are the querent's possible goal or destiny and his or her hopes and ideals related?

Q3 Consider the Tower in position six, future influences, and Strength in position seven, negative feelings. What interpretation would you give?

Q4 If Death is in position six, the area of future influences, what significance would this have on the querent's negative feelings if Judgment appears in position seven?

Q5 What factors would you consider important for a reading if the Emperor were chosen for position seven, negative feelings, and Strength for position eight, family and friends?

Q6 How would you interpret the Sun in position seven, negative feelings, and Temperance in position eight, family and friends?

Q7 Assess the Moon in position seven and the Devil in position nine. How do you think these cards interact to reflect the querent's negative feelings and hopes and ideals?

Q8 What are the querent's negative feelings and hopes and ideals if the Chariot appears in position seven and Temperance in position nine?

Q9 Interpret the querent's negative feelings if Temperance lies in position seven. How would this be affected by the Lovers in position nine, the area reflecting the querent's hopes and ideals?

Q10 Would the Empress in position eight, family and friends, and the Hierophant in position nine, hopes and ideals, have any bearing on each other?

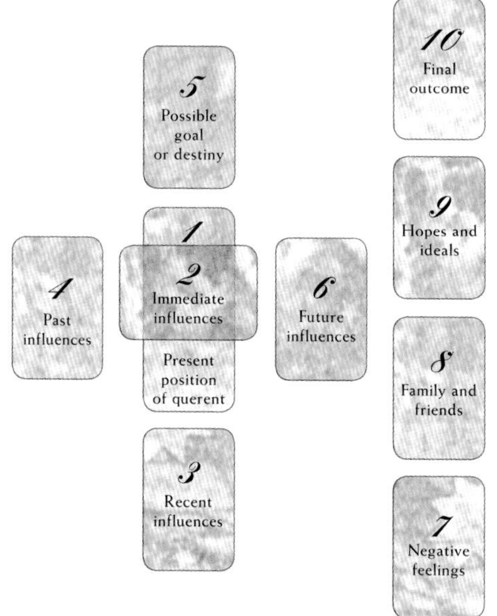

MAJOR ARCANA: FEELINGS ANSWERS

A1 Judgment denotes justified pride and rewards for past efforts. In position five, possible goal or destiny, it tells the querent that creative efforts from the past should be reused in an interesting new concept. In position eight, family and friends, the World means that, provided the querent accepts that the opinions of others are equally valid, a creative venture, possibly with a friend or relation, will make a dream come true.

A2 When in position five, possible goal or destiny, the Chariot means that a triumphant reward will come from artistic work as long as problems are recognized and solved successfully. The Star in position nine, hopes and ideals, denotes that a matter or problem requiring a firm decision from the querent will bring peace of mind but must be dealt with soon.

A3 The Tower symbolizes a sudden catastrophe, shock, or a disruption of life's pattern that in the future will prove beneficial and enlightening. In position six, future influences, it tells the querent to see things as they really are and not as they are wanted to be. Strength in position seven, negative feelings, reveals that the querent is giving too much of his or her time to too many negative people, who are draining the querent's energy. The querent should think more about his or her own needs.

A4 Death symbolizes change and transformation, and that a negative period in life is over and a triumph is coming. In position six, future influences, it denotes that contentment, progress, and success will come with a new view of life. In position seven, negative feelings, Judgment means that self-healing comes from self-honesty and the realization that past failures may have been caused by the querent's own faults or weaknesses. However, happiness and success will eventually come from a neglected talent.

A5 In position seven, negative feelings, the Emperor reminds the querent never to doubt him or herself or lose a sense of adventure. It also indicates that past kindness to others will be repaid. Strength in position eight, family and friends, tells the querent not to listen to others when offered a new direction in life but to remember how his or her courage overcame challenges in the past.

A6 The Sun is a joyous card. In position seven, negative feelings, it tells the querent that happiness lies within if you can learn to accept your faults, appreciate your virtues, and be honest about what you want in life. Temperance means that combining the spiritual with the material results in peace and harmony. In position eight, family and friends, it indicates that an offer of a business partnership or a marriage proposal will be made by a wealthy person.

Happiness lies within if you can learn to accept your faults, appreciate your virtues, and be honest about what you want in life.

A7 The Moon in position seven, negative feelings, reveals that self-deception can arise from an overdeveloped imagination and warns the querent to see things for what they really are. The Devil denotes a life ruled by physical appetites, but also a life-changing event. In position nine, hopes and ideals, it reinforces the Moon by telling the querent that accepting one's own faults and virtues will lead to tolerance and an understanding of other people.

A8 The Chariot is a positive card and can mean patience, endurance, wealth, and triumph over problems. In position seven, negative feelings, it denotes the arrival of calm after a storm. Temperance in position nine, hopes and ideals, indicates that success will come to the querent, who manages things skillfully because of vitality, mental agility, moderation, and adaptability.

A9 Temperance denotes peace and future harmony and the combination of the spiritual and the material. In position seven, negative feelings, it warns that if the querent wants relationships to last, feelings such as love, respect, and affection that have been repressed must now be revealed. The Lovers in position nine, hopes and ideals, indicates that a sudden flash of insight will solve a long-standing problem.

A10 The Empress in position eight, family and friends, denotes that real love encourages people to be themselves. This means that the querent must never try to criticize or control his or her partner if they are both to be happy. The Hierophant in position nine, hopes and ideals, tells the querent that fulfillment will come from an occupation or profession that will uplift and help others.

Spiritual, emotional, and financial wealth are predicted by Temperance in position eight, family and friends, and could indicate a proposal of marriage.

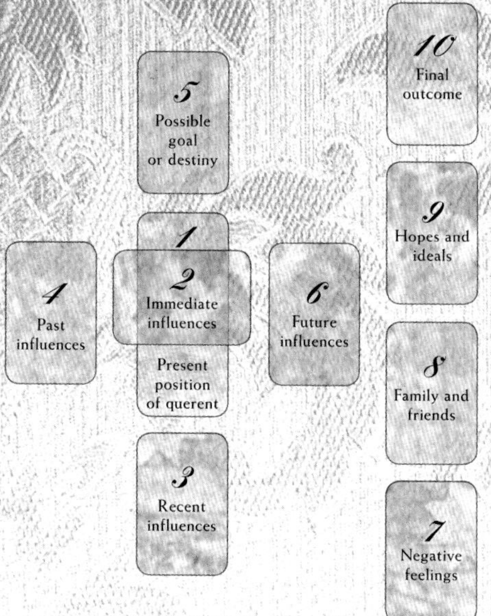

MAJOR ARCANA: FINAL OUTCOME QUESTIONS

These questions look at combinations of Major Arcana cards and concentrate on position ten, signifying the final outcome. Refer to page 22-23 for instructions on how to perform the Celtic Cross; see pages 154-158 for the answers to these questions.

Q1 How would the final outcome of the reading be affected if the Tower appears in position ten and the Empress in position five, representing the querent's possible goal or destiny?

Q2 If the Tower appears in position seven, negative feelings, and the Chariot in position ten, final outcome, how would you interpret them?

Q3 Imagine a reading in which the Chariot occurs in position seven, negative feelings, and then consider the Fool in position ten, final outcome. What would you say to the querent?

Q4 If Justice appears in position eight, family and friends, what bearing would this have on the final outcome if the High Priestess appears in position ten?

Q5 What final outcome would you give for a reading in which Judgment lies in position eight, family and friends, and the World in position ten?

Q6 Consider how Judgment could be interpreted in position nine, symbolizing the querent's hopes and ideals. If the Magician is chosen for position ten, what would be the final outcome and what effect would the two cards have on each other?

Q7 How would you interpret the Fool in position nine, hopes and ideals, and the Hierophant in position ten, final outcome?

Q8 Does the Sun in position nine and the Lovers in position ten indicate that the querent's hopes and ideals will be fulfilled in the final outcome?

Q9 How do the High Priestess in position nine, hopes and ideals, and the Wheel of Fortune in position ten, final outcome, interact?

Q10 If the Tower and the Star appear in positions nine and ten respectively, what hopes, ideals, and final outcome would you foresee for the querent?

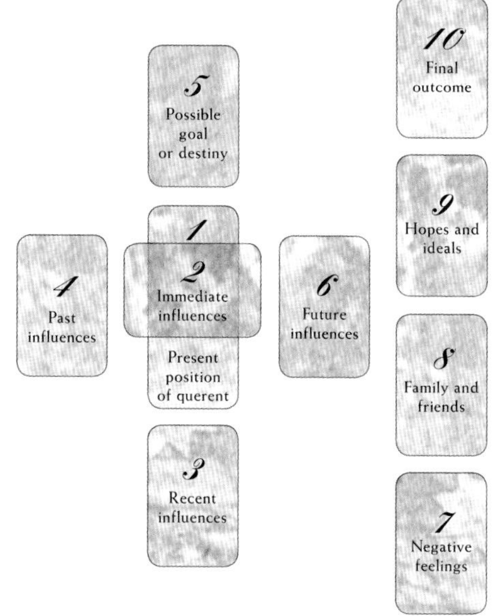

Major Arcana: Final Outcome answers

A1 The Empress in position five, possible goal or destiny, shows that past efforts bring recognition and reward and past kindnesses bring help. The Tower in position ten, final outcome, symbolizes that life will be altered by an unexpected and painful event that is both hurtful and shocking but will eventually bring happiness. However, when these two cards are opposite each other in the fifth and tenth positions, they cancel each other out.

A2 The Tower in position seven, negative feelings, shows that an unexpected conflict will strip away all the querent's pretence and, through self-honesty and courage, eventually lead to a realistic acceptance of life. In position ten, final outcome, the Chariot symbolizes honor and recognition and possibly the chance of swift, luxurious travel connected with career.

A3 The Chariot in position seven, negative feelings, symbolizes peace after strife, triumph over problems, and psychological or physical healing. The Fool can represent spiritual protection as a result of learning life's lessons, and courage and wisdom needed when making important choices. When in position ten, final outcome, it shows that spiritual peace and happiness will come to the querent as a result of making the correct decision.

A4 Justice denotes a well-balanced, honest person with integrity, and when in position eight, family and friends, means that whatever the querent has given in the past will be returned a thousandfold, in a surprising way or from an unexpected source. The High Priestess symbolizes inner perception, spiritual enlightenment, and protection. When in position ten, final outcome, it indicates that lasting happiness will come to the querent from both spiritual and worldly triumphs.

A5 Judgment can mean the end of one period of life and the beginning of another, and indicates that the querent should not be afraid of change. The fact that it is in position eight, family and friends, could reveal that the querent is too dependent on other people to want to make a change. The World in position ten, final outcome, denotes a lesson learned and a dream come true. It shows that the querent will have the strength to do what should be done to achieve contentment.

A6 In position nine, hopes and ideals, Judgment shows that the future is becoming clearer now that the querent is beginning to see things as they really are. In position ten, final outcome, the Magician denotes a new beginning coming after a creative success, but it warns that true happiness will come to the querent only after attaining self-knowledge.

The Chariot in position ten, final outcome, can indicate a high-powered career that will involve swift travel in first-class luxury.

A7 The Fool represents spiritual progress, learning life's lessons, and risk through recklessness. In position nine, hopes and ideals, it tells the querent to trust in him or herself and have courage when starting a new life because it will bring happiness. The Hierophant in position ten, final outcome, teaches that real success will only come when one lives with the courage of one's own convictions.

A8 The Sun in position nine, hopes and ideals, says there will be a triumph, either from work already done or someone who is coming into the querent's life. In position ten, final outcome, the Lovers indicates that the querent has at last learned how to choose wisely.

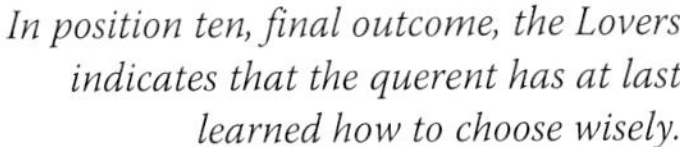
In position ten, final outcome, the Lovers indicates that the querent has at last learned how to choose wisely.

A9 In position nine, hopes and ideals, the High Priestess reveals that artistic success will be achieved because of inner commitment and spiritual strength. The Wheel of Fortune in position ten, final outcome, signifies that if the querent grasps an opportunity that is coming, there will be success. Also, coming next to the High Priestess, it can mean a lawsuit that brings victory and recompense.

A10 The Tower in position nine, hopes and ideals, indicates that no matter how painful past losses were, they must be accepted and not relived constantly if the querent wants to be free in mind, body, and spirit. The Star is always a welcome card to appear in position ten, final outcome. It reveals that, despite past pain and loss, a decision or a new direction that has been taken or is about to be taken will bring the querent true love, lasting peace, and happiness.

The Chariot in position seven, negative feelings, reveals that the querent will eventually defeat physical or psychological problems. When combined with the Fool in position ten, final outcome, the cards indicate that regaining spiritual strength will quicken the healing process.

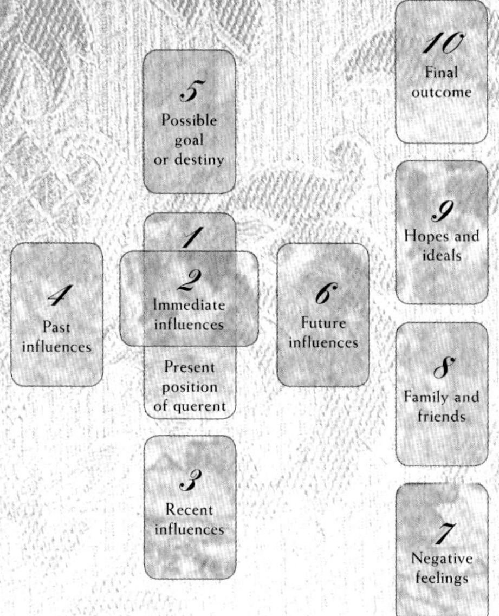

Minor Arcana: General Questions

These questions look at Minor Arcana cards appearing in conjunction with Major Arcana cards and concentrate on positions one to nine, signifying the various influences affecting the querent and his or her feelings. Refer to page 22-23 for instructions on how to perform the Celtic Cross; see pages 164-169 for the answers to these questions.

Q1 What does the Three of Wands in position one indicate about the querent and his or her present position, and how do the immediate influences represented by the High Priestess in position two affect the querent?

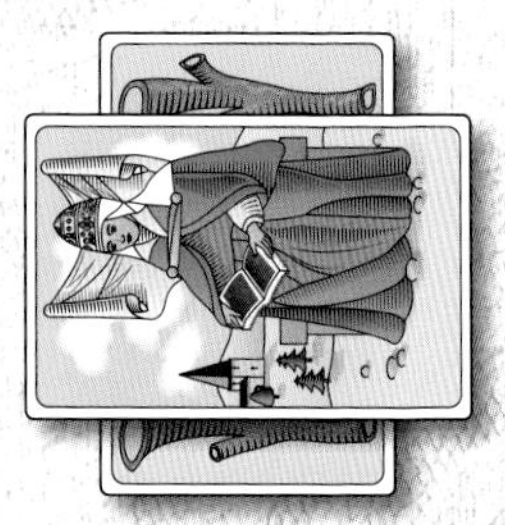

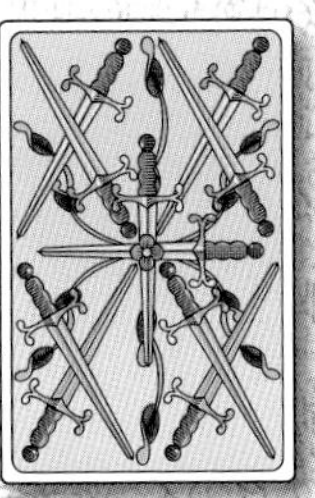

Q2 How would you interpret Strength in position three, recent influences, and the Ten of Swords in position four, past influences?

Q3 What effect are recent and past influences having on the querent if the Lovers appears in position three and the Ace of Cups in position four? Q3 Imagine a reading in which the Chariot occurs in position seven, negative feelings, and then consider the Fool in position ten, final outcome. What would you say to the querent?

Q4 Assess the Five of Pentacles in position four and Judgment in position six. What do these cards reveal about the past and future influences on the querent?

Q5 If the Wheel of Fortune is chosen for position six, future influences, does this imply that the querent's hopes and ideals, as represented by the Five of Cups in position nine, will be achieved?

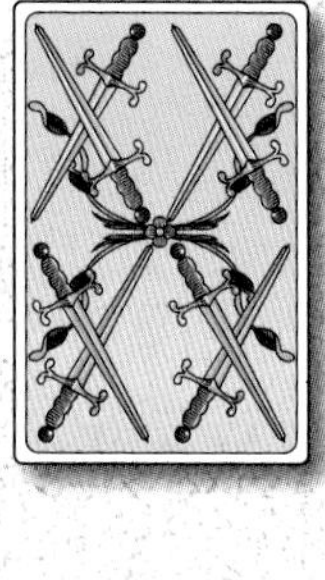

Q6 If the Hanged Man is in position seven, negative feelings, and the Eight of Swords is in position eight, family and friends, what interpretation would you give to the querent?

Q7 What meanings would you give to the World in position seven, negative feelings, and the Ten of Pentacles in position eight, family and friends?

Q8 If the Four of Cups lies in position seven and the Emperor in position eight, how would you assess the querent's negative feelings and the effect of his or her family and friends on those feelings?

Q9 How do the Moon in position eight, family and friends, and the Ace of Wands in position nine, hopes and ideals, affect each other?

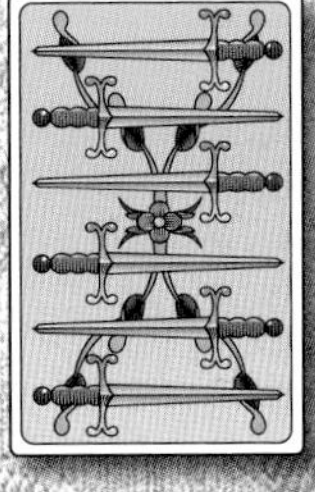

Q10 Would you give a positive or negative interpretation in relation to family and friends and hopes and ideals if the Hanged Man appears in position eight and the Six of Swords in position nine?

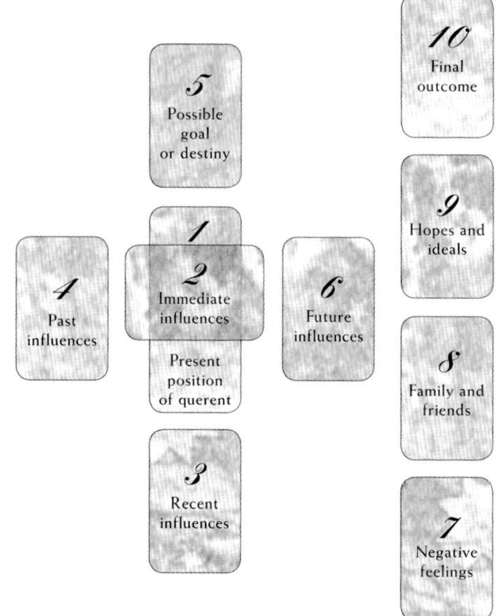

MINOR ARCANA: GENERAL ANSWERS

A1 The card in position one can describe both the querent and his or her present position. The Three of Wands symbolizes an artist or inventor who has powerful convictions, strong and original expressive abilities, and produces inspirational and original work that results in success and recognition. The card also signifies creative or artistic ideas coming to fruition, help from a powerful associate, or a partnership resulting in wealth and fame. The High Priestess in position two, immediate influences, possesses the basic meanings of learning, spiritual protection, and mystery, but also indicates creative talents and cultural advancement, which strengthens the meaning of the previous card. The High Priestess in this particular position also implies that a caring person will give the querent generous help that will enable the querent to develop his or her psychic sense, or more importantly here, unrecognized or neglected creative talent.

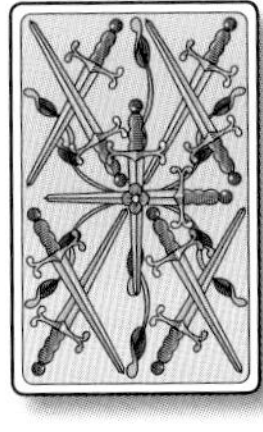

A2 The Ten of Swords in position four, past influences, symbolizes a national depression or the lowest ebb in human affairs, during which time the querent has, for the first time, seen something for what it really is, not what it may have originally seemed to be. This has helped the querent to achieve self-honesty, self-acceptance, and integrity. Although the Ten of Swords has some negative implications, here it is favorably aspected by the presence of Strength in position three, recent influences. This emphasizes the more positive interpretations of the Ten of Swords, which include the end of spiritual darkness and rebirth. Strength has no negative meanings, and as well as affecting the cards around it, also influences the whole reading. It symbolizes wise use of power, courage, love conquering hate, and the spiritual conquering the material. It can also mean that a life-changing opportunity is coming that must be taken. When Strength is in position three, it underlines this latter meaning because it says that an offer is coming that could change the querent's life for the better, resulting in happiness, reward, and future recognition.

A3 The Ace of Cups in position four, past influences, denotes a romantic meeting that can end in a love affair as well as joy in artistic work, deep faith, spiritual nourishment, happy news, and congenial company. When it appears near other cards symbolizing love—as it does in this instance coming after the Lovers—it signifies a marriage. The Lovers can indicate that a choice must be made between physical and idealistic love, or love and career, using intuition to make the right decision. If this happens, friendship, affection, and harmony will follow. Here, in position three, recent influences, the Lovers teaches that relationships with other people can make us aware of our own personal failings and shows us the necessity for self-control. The querent should listen to this warning if the marriage indicated by the Ace of Cups is going to be happy.

A4 The Five of Pentacles in position four, past influences, is not a happy card because it means loss in many ways, such as loss of judgment, work, position, home, or lover. It also represents sorrow and disappointment, spiritual loneliness, and enforced restrictions. On a more positive note, it can indicate that lasting friendships can be made with people in similar circumstances, and when it appears near positive cards such as Judgment, it can also mean that self-confidence will be regained and there will be an opportunity to start anew. Judgment itself symbolizes the ending of one period of life and the beginning of another, change and renewal, release, rewards for past efforts, and a mental awakening that leads to prestige and success. In position six, future influences, the latter interpretation is emphasized because it signifies that a sudden change or mental awakening will bring new viewpoints and new creative efforts. These in turn will bring a sense of happiness and fulfillment to the querent.

A5 The Wheel of Fortune can mean a sudden change, sometimes as the result of past efforts, that is usually for the better, and if there are problems, delays, or setbacks, they will in time prove beneficial. When in position six, future influences, it tells the querent that happiness and maturity will come from different methods or ways of thinking, or taking a different direction in life or work. The Five of Cups in position nine, hopes and ideals, indicates something that has or is about to come to an end, sadness through a loss or mistake, parting with a lover, or regrettable behavior in the past. It also warns the querent never to ignore spiritual needs. It echoes the message conveyed by the Wheel of Fortune, because it means something new beginning, new paths about to be taken, and a new life about to start that will bring happiness.

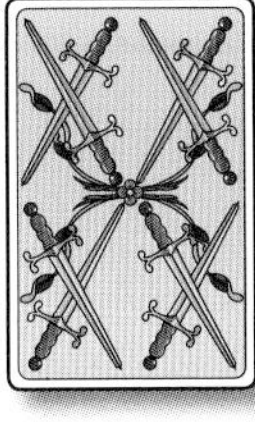

A6 The Hanged Man can symbolize a willing sacrifice, suffering, hardship, or loss. It can also represent a decision or forgiveness that brings wisdom and peace, inner strength, and the reversal of a way of life. In position seven, negative feelings, it implies that irresponsibility and negative thoughts and actions can undermine security and spoil the future. The Eight of Swords in position eight, family and friends, has a similar meaning, in that it signifies that lack of confidence, negativity, self-deception, and hypocrisy can all cause indecision, and that self-honesty, confidence, and attention to detail are necessary to bring about changes and avoid criticism. However, it also reveals that bonds will soon be broken and restrictions lifted, and should the next card be a positive one, it means hurts will be healed, self-confidence will return, and progress will be made by the querent.

The Wheel of Fortune in position six, future influences, signifies that the querent is about to be subjected to the vagaries of fate but these will eventually prove beneficial.

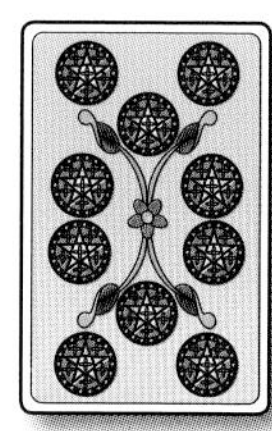

A7 The World is the material wish card, symbolizing dreams coming true, joy, happiness, both spiritual and material reward, and sometimes traveling long distances across water. In position seven, negative feelings, it says that support will be gained if the querent's ambitions and dreams are shared with the people who care and are close by. The Ten of Pentacles in position eight, family and friends, is also a positive card, meaning creative achievements bringing rewards and material, spiritual, and creative wealth being shared with others. It is the family card, representing respect for history, a settled way of life, establishing new traditions, blood ties, inheritance, dowries, legacies, and purchase or sale of property. So it seems that a loving family and close friends will encourage and help the strong and generous querent to be happy, wealthy, and successful.

A8 The Four of Cups in position seven, negative feelings, reveals that the querent is both discontented with life at present and feels unfulfilled. The result will be a period of self-searching before the querent takes a new direction in life or starts a new career. It carries the warning that the querent must trust his or her own intuition or inner voice, because meddling from jealous or hostile people could ruin a friendship or a budding romance. The Emperor denotes worldly wealth, power, and authority, self-discipline, intellectual ability, knowledge through experience, creative talent, mental activity, and passion and romance. Its presence in the spread indicates that the querent will be helped to achieve success in a new direction by a powerful friend or a governmental agency of some kind. However, when in position eight, family and friends, it also signifies that being strong can sometimes seem like a punishment because you can become burdened by other people's troubles, and the querent would therefore be well advised to say no more often to friends and relations.

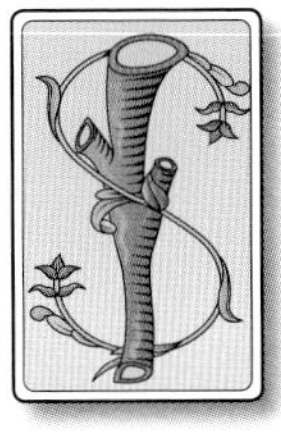

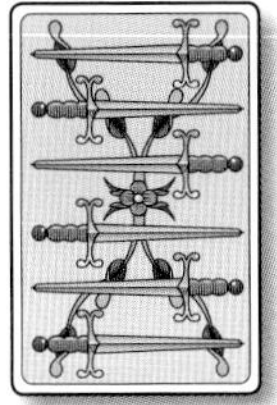

A9 The Moon can signify an emotional crisis, storms weathered, deception, a loved one's misfortune, intuition, and creativity. In position eight, family and friends, it also carries a warning for the querent who, having learned many lessons both from previous actions and relationships, needs to be reminded not to make the same mistakes again by forgetting what happened in the past. The Ace of Wands in position nine, hopes and ideals, is a happy card. It reveals that a renewal of the querent's energy and new wisdom or knowledge will bring dissatisfaction with the present circumstances or attitude to life, but a new beginning or foundation will follow that results in contentment and success as well as inspiration or innovation, bringing a new creative cycle.

A10 The Hanged Man in position eight, family and friends, symbolizes a willing sacrifice that causes suffering, loss, or hardship, forgiveness bringing wisdom, and a decision that leads to spiritual peace, inner strength, and a reversal of a way of life. So after a sacrifice and hardship, the querent must be considering a change of life and work. The Six of Swords in position nine, hopes and ideals, is the card of flight or travel, but also denotes many different kinds of change. This may be to a better environment, a new career, the end of a difficult time, success coming after anxiety, obstacles removed after a stressful time, or an overseas visitor bringing good news. It also carries the message that risk brings rewards and tells the querent not to be afraid to find a new home or to seek more satisfying work.

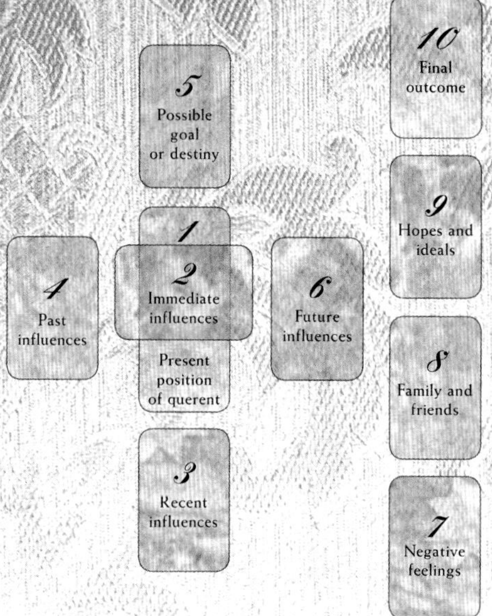

MINOR ARCANA: FINAL OUTCOME QUESTIONS

These questions look at Minor Arcana cards appearing in conjunction with Major Arcana cards and concentrate on position ten, the final outcome. Refer to page 22-23 for instructions on how to perform the Celtic Cross; see pages 174–180 for the answers to these questions.

Q1 Do the Ten of Wands in position five, possible goal or destiny, and Death in position ten, final outcome, have any effect on each other?

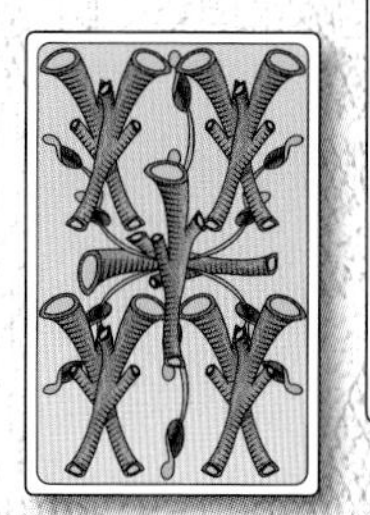

Q2 How would you interpret the Seven of Cups in position five, possible goal or destiny, and the Chariot in position ten, final outcome?

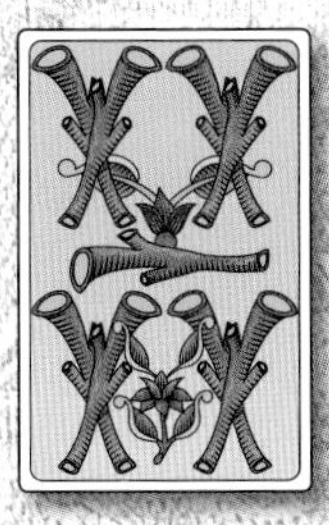

Q3 If the Nine of Wands appears in position five and the Emperor in position ten, would this indicate that the querent's possible goal or destiny and final outcome are the same?

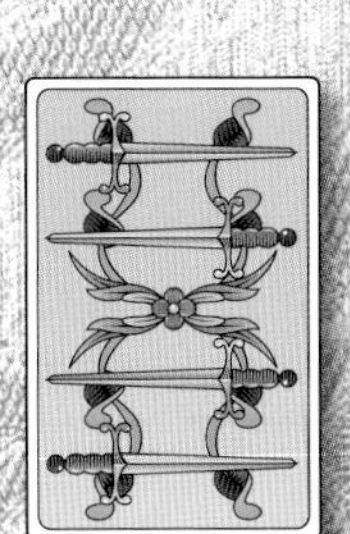

Q4 What effect does the Four of Swords in position six, future influences, have on the final outcome, represented by the Star in position ten?

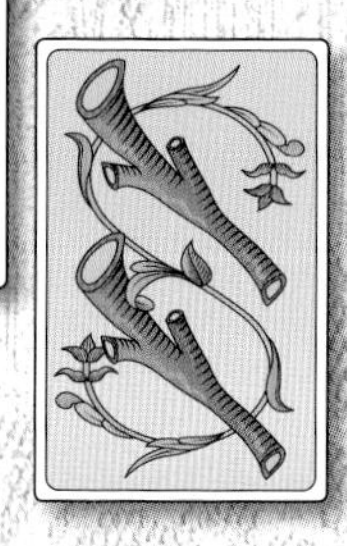

Q5 How will the querent's negative feelings, symbolized by the Two of Wands in position seven, affect the final outcome, represented by Judgment in position ten?

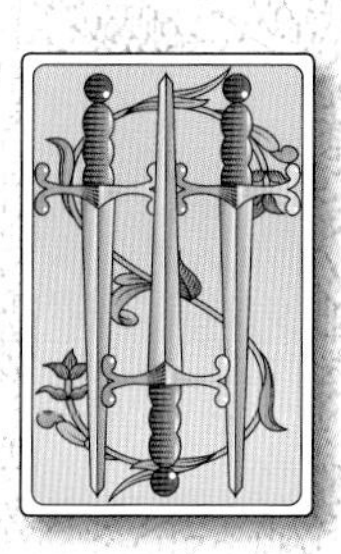

Q6 The Three of Swords in position eight symbolizes the querent's family and friends. Will this have a positive or negative effect on Temperance in position ten, signifying the final outcome?

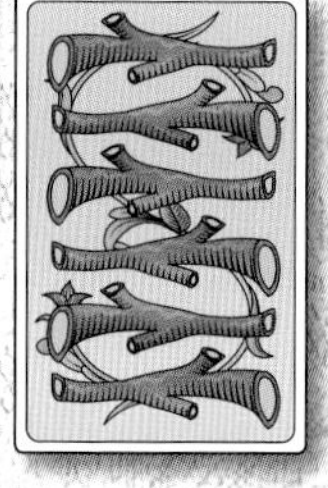

Q7 Consider how the Six of Wands could be interpreted in position nine, hopes and ideals. If the Devil appears in position ten, what would the final outcome be and how would the two cards affect each other?

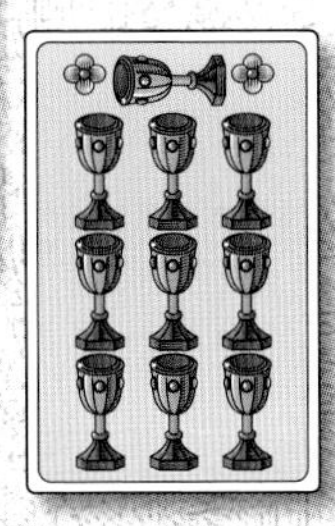

Q8 Do the Ten of Cups in position nine and the Sun in position ten indicate that the querent's hopes and ideals will be fulfilled in the final outcome?

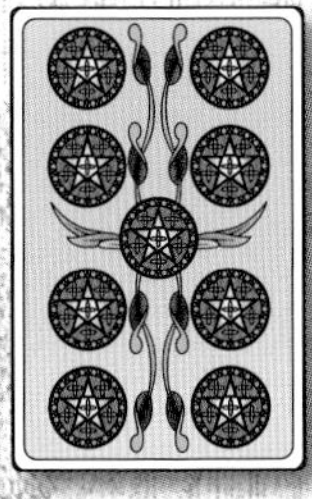

Q9 How would you interpret the Moon in position nine, hopes and ideals, and the Nine of Pentacles in position ten, final outcome?

Q10 Consider the combination of the Two of Pentacles in position nine and the Fool in position ten. What meaning would you attribute to them with regard to the querent's hopes and ideals and the final outcome?

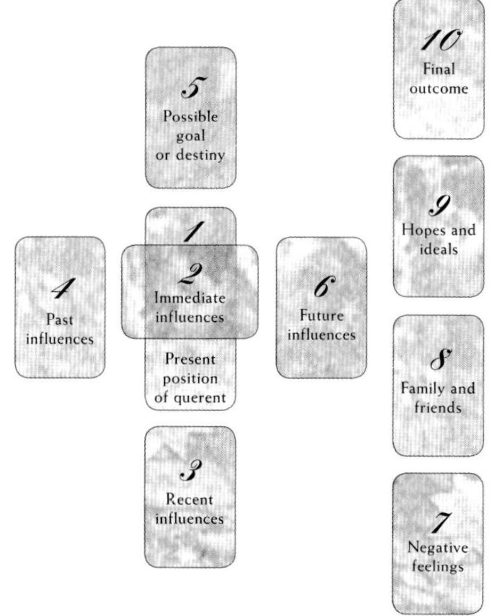

MINOR ARCANA: FINAL OUTCOME ANSWERS

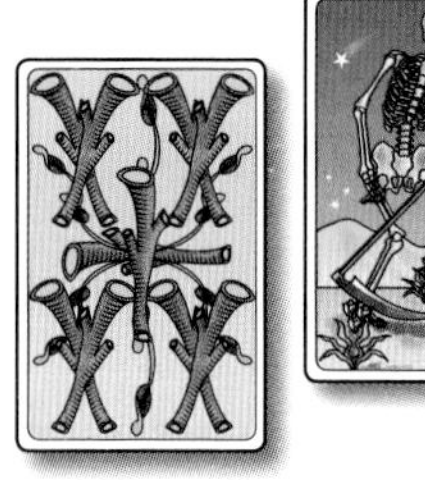

A1 The Ten of Wands in position five, possible goal or destiny, means that burdens affecting the querent will soon be lifted and problems solved. However, it also warns that narrow-minded or fixed ideas must be discarded if the querent is to succeed in a new direction.
If this is done, the querent will be rewarded with new contracts, new ventures, consolidation, big business, and a possible overseas journey or a trip to a strange place. Death can symbolize a shock or destruction that leads to a transformation, the end of a troublesome period of life, or an artistic or creative struggle leading to success and triumph. When in position ten, final outcome, it indicates that

the querent's insecurity, intolerance, pretensions, and materialism have dissipated like the darkness at dawn and the future is like the warm sun on the horizon: clear, bright, and golden.

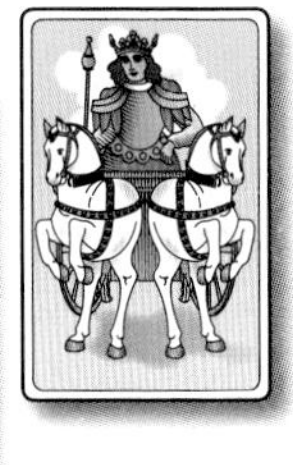

A2 The Seven of Cups in position five, possible goal or destiny, predicts that the querent will receive an exceptional and unexpected offer that could fulfill a dream but that wisdom will be required to make the right choice. It also symbolizes mental ability, creative inspiration that could result in unexpected rewards, and mystical experiences. The Chariot can represent wealth, prestige, success resulting from patience and endurance, and sustained effort that conquers stressful problems and difficulties. In position ten, final outcome, the Chariot signifies that an opportunity for luxurious travel could be coming, connected with work, but more importantly, the querent's career will bring honor and recognition.

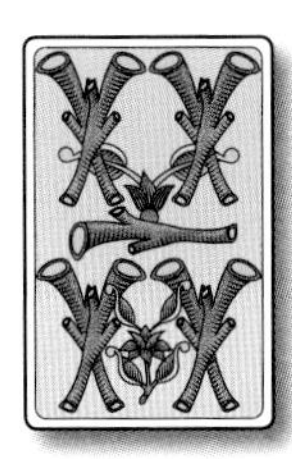

A3 The Nine of Wands is the strength card of the Minor Arcana. It is a good card to appear in position five, possible goal or destiny, because it symbolizes balanced judgment, a trusting nature, sound advice given or taken, strength and integrity bringing lasting triumph, a victory after a final challenge, courage in defense, strength in reserve, and success or expansion in professional or artistic fields. The Emperor means worldly authority, power, wealth, intellect, mental activity, knowledge through experience, self-discipline, and creative ability. When in position ten, it also denotes a new and rewarding opportunity in business, a successful official position, or a high government post. So it is clear that the final outcome is exactly what the querent desires, and with hard work, good judgment, and integrity, he or she will achieve great success.

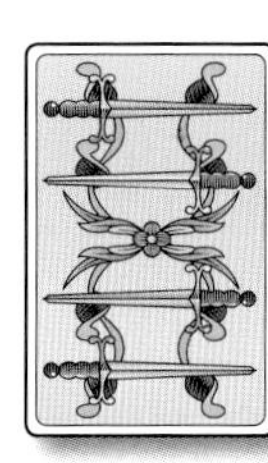

A4 The Four of Swords in position six, future influences, can signify a retreat after a testing time in order to think things through, peace and order coming after struggle or chaos, and hospitalization or convalescence. The Star can represent the refreshment of both mind and spirit after a troubled time, spiritual inspiration, support, and unselfish help given by friends. In position ten, final outcome, it also means that, despite pain or loss, a new decision or a new direction already taken or about to be taken by the querent will bring inner peace, a love that is genuine, and great happiness.

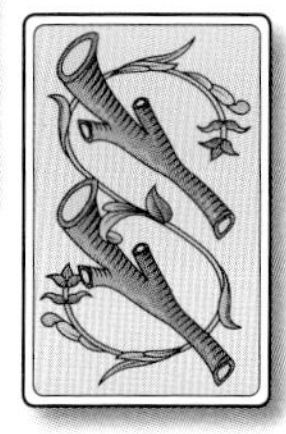

A5 The Two of Wands is a positive card to have in position seven, negative feelings, for it means high motives, courage, willpower, initiative, intellectual work, justice, tolerance, obstacles overcome by strength, and help from those in authority. It shows that the querent has gained maturity, inner strength, and wisdom, which has helped to minimize negative feelings and will lead to future happiness and lasting success. Judgment is a strong card that indicates the end of one period of life and the beginning of another, release or change and renewal, rewards for past efforts with justified pride in them, or a mental awakening that will bring fame and success. When in position ten, final outcome, it tells the querent that with determination and self-belief, he or she will find the courage to take the right path. It carries the positive message that the sun is beginning to shine through the clouds and will light up the road the querent should take and show the way forward.

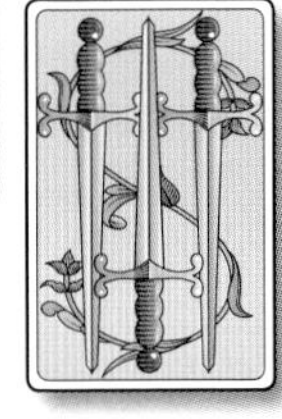

a balanced attitude to life, and good financial sense. It is also symbolic of future harmony and peace. In position ten, final outcome, it tells the querent not to worry because when one of life's chapters closes, another always opens.

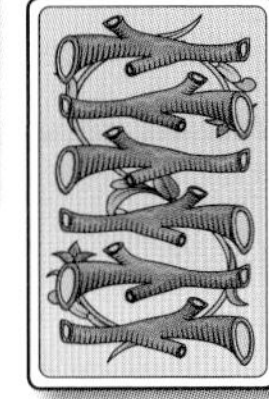

A6 The Three of Swords in position eight, family and friends, is a negative card that denotes temporary or permanent separation, a partnership broken, or a marriage dissolved. This will cause upheaval, disruption, and pain but will be followed by healing and the sense that the ground has been cleared for something better. Temperance, a positive card, means compromise, moderation, learning to combine the material with the spiritual to achieve

A7 The Six of Wands in position nine, hopes and ideals, is the career card of the Minor Arcana, representing satisfaction, triumphant achievement, fulfillment of ambitions, victory over difficulties, diplomacy conquering opposition, a major problem solved, wonderful news, and public acclaim. It also warns that the envy of others may spoil the querent's triumph. The Devil is a negative card, meaning a life dominated by physical appetite and materialism, or a strong power used negatively or unwisely. It

The Star in position ten, final outcome, reveals that the querent can rely on unselfish support from friends in a time of crisis.

also symbolizes a sudden inexorable event or change of life that can be either positive or negative, depending on the cards near it. However, in this case the event will obviously be a positive one because the Devil is favorably aspected by the Six of Wands in position nine. The final outcome therefore indicates that life will suddenly change for the querent and he or she must be ready to accept what is offered and be ready to enjoy it.

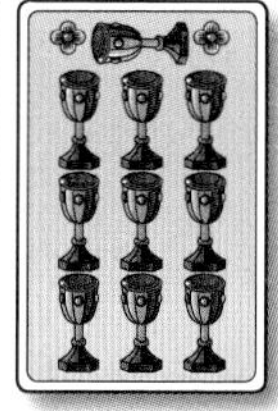

A8 The Ten of Cups in position nine, hopes and ideals, is a positive card. It symbolizes honor, prestige, lasting success, spiritual happiness, peace, the love of friends, work in a public sphere, prestige and publicity, buying or selling, successful legal matters concerning residence or property, and a journey with a happy ending. The Sun denotes a successful achievement against all odds, an ambition realized, health, energy, and material comfort. So it is clear that the querent will enjoy future success in business, a happy and prosperous life, and many loving friends because he or she possesses the gift of gratitude. Although it may take time, the Sun in position ten, final outcome, reveals that although the querent may feel that the hard work and struggle currently being experienced seems unending, personal happiness and joy will definitely come in the future.

The querent will enjoy future success in business, a happy and prosperous life, and many loving friends because he or she possesses the gift of gratitude.

The purchase of a residence could be indicated by the Ten of Cups in position nine, hopes and ideals. With the Sun in position ten, final outcome, this will be a happy move that is both uplifting and peaceful.

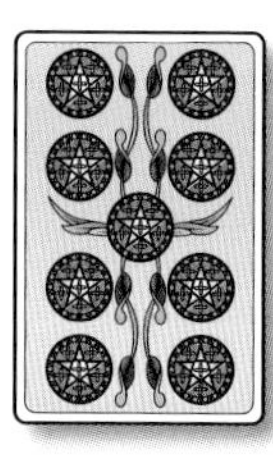

A9 The Moon means a loved one's misfortune, uncertainty, deception, hidden forces, imagination, dreams, the subconscious, and creativity. In position nine, hopes and ideals, it also says that the subconscious is fueling the imagination and together they will create a powerful work that will bring both spiritual growth and wealth to the querent. The Nine of Pentacles in position ten, final outcome, denotes that the querent is a unique, independent, and talented person who will in the future earn a substantial income through sensible administration and consistent effort, and receive a reward from a finished project or find a solution to a problem. However, despite the promised success, it also warns the querent that inner satisfaction and peace can only come through self-knowledge and that the querent has to learn this lesson.

A10 The Two of Pentacles in position nine, hopes and ideals, symbolizes imminent changes, harmony, and good management in the midst of sudden financial or domestic upheaval. It also indicates that new moves need to be made. Its other meanings include literary ability, success in one direction, and reward from using one talent as well as a move or journey to a new country or home. The Fool represents spiritual strength and protection as life's lessons are learned, and important choices or changes that require courage and wisdom. When in position ten, final outcome, it also signifies that successful achievements, spiritual peace, and happiness will result from making the right decision. So the querent will achieve success and happiness by making the right changes or new moves in career and life.

When in position ten, final outcome, it also signifies that successful achievements, spiritual peace, and happiness will result from making the right decision.

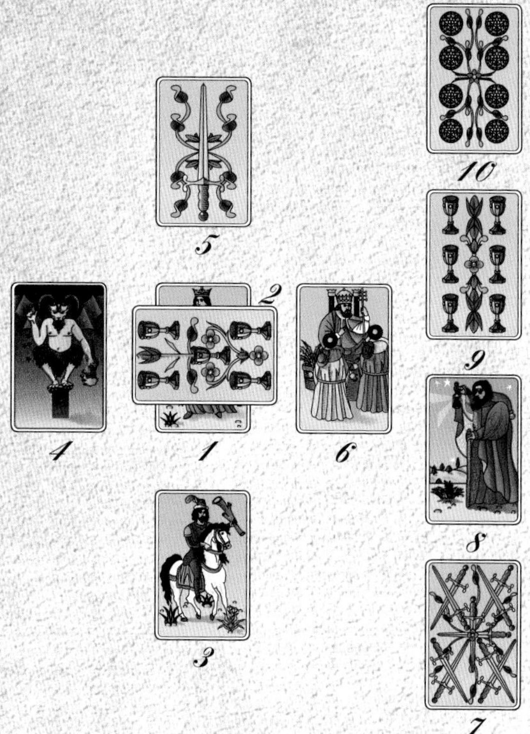

Full Reading

This is an example of a full reading using the Celtic Cross (see page 22-23 for instructions). Remember to start by looking at the card in position ten, then check the card in position five because sometimes these two cards cancel each other out. Next, look at the remaining positions, paying particular attention to strongly positive or negative cards.

10: Final Outcome

The Eight of Pentacles is the talent and energy card of the tarot. It reveals that a well-paid profession will come from recently discovered or developed skills.

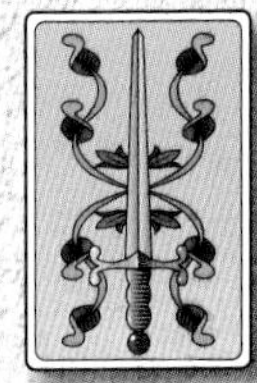

5: Possible Goal or Destiny

The Ace of Swords means divine justice, a strong force for good or ill, strength in adversity, triumph over obstacles, and even more importantly here, a sense of the inevitable—something that cannot be stopped that will change the querent's perspective on life.

1: Present Position of Querent

The Queen of Cups represents a romantic, intuitive, artistically gifted and loving wife or mistress, an idealist practicing what she preaches, a mother, a new romance, new horizons, or new beginnings.

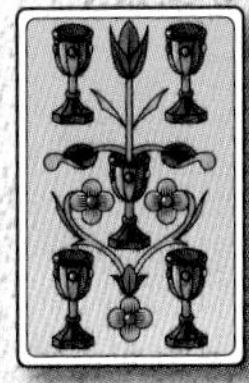

2: Immediate Influences

The Five of Cups symbolizes a crossroads in life, something ended, something new beginning, new paths about to be taken, mistakes made, a love affair finished, and regrets after loss or bad behavior. It also carries the warning that spiritual needs and the inner voice must not be ignored.

3: Recent Influences

The Knight of Wands represents a volatile, lovable, charming man between the ages of 21 and 35 who likes travel and change. It can also denote a flight, journey, change of residence, and good financial ability.

4: Past Influences

The Devil symbolizes a life dominated by physical appetites or material gain, a strong power used negatively, and a sudden inexorable event. Here, it indicates that real progress will only be made if the querent replaces negative habits or influences with positive actions and thoughts.

6: Future Influences

The Hierophant can signify craving for social approval, religion, conventionality, self-honesty, spirituality, or hidden secrets revealed. In this position, it indicates that success will not be won or ambitions fulfilled without efficiency, organization, hard work, realistic assessment, and self-honesty.

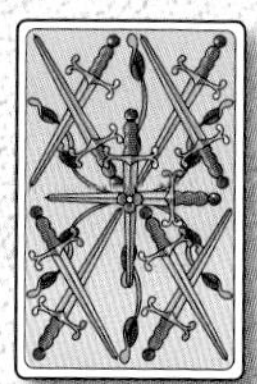

7: Negative Feelings

The Ten of Swords represents the lowest point in both human and national affairs, but also means that for the first time there is self-honesty and something is seen clearly for what it is and not what it seems to be. Positively aspected, as it is here next to the Hermit in position eight, it also symbolizes self-acceptance and the end of spiritual darkness bringing a rebirth.

8: Family and Friends

The Hermit denotes caution when choosing a new path, wise counsel, an enlightening journey, and sudden insight solving a problem. Here, it strengthens the meaning of the Ten of Swords in position seven, as it emphasizes that understanding others and gaining friends comes from recognizing one's own faults and realizing that others also have problems.

9: Hopes and Ideals

The Six of Cups signifies benefits from past efforts, the reappearance of old friends, and a long-held ambition realized. It also has a warning not to live in the past.

Interpretation

The querent's past life has been dominated by physical appetites and material gain. A sudden event has brought trouble and loss, and progress can only be made if negative habits are replaced with positive ones. While it is obvious that the querent is still paying for mistakes, it is also clear that he or she has the strength to triumph over obstacles. With self-honesty, hard work, and a realistic outlook, the querent will eventually be able to achieve success in a new profession, possibly concerned with finance. The querent now also recognizes that others also have problems and will receive some sound advice from either an old or new friend.

The cards in this spread reveal that, if the querent abandons negative attitudes and nurtures friendships, personal satisfaction and financial security will be the rewards.

The Tarot Deck

This chapter is a quick-reference guide to the meanings of each tarot card. The meanings of the Major Arcana cards are listed first, including significant combinations, followed by the four suits of the Minor Arcana. Try learning the meanings of one card each night, or you may find it useful to copy them onto labels that you can tape to the backs of your tarot cards until you become more confident of them.

The Major Arcana

The Major Arcana are the 22 picture cards of the tarot and are believed to describe humankind's spiritual journey through life. When a large number of Major Arcana cards appear in a spread, they overshadow the meanings of the Minor Arcana cards that accompany them, and denote significant events in the querent's life. Each card has a name and is numbered from 1 to 21, with the Fool either unnumbered and placed last in the deck, or labeled zero and placed first.

0 THE FOOL

The blithe spirit or eternal traveler.

One of the most significant cards in the tarot, the Fool is searching for the secrets of life, adopting, abandoning, embracing, or discarding experiences to attain perfection. It denotes that the querent is spiritually guided and protected, a blithe spirit who will face a choice of vital importance or a change that requires great wisdom and courage. There is also the warning of carelessness, risk through recklessness, heedlessness, the unexpected, and sudden travel.

Combinations The Fool is a highly spiritual card and its meaning is canceled when powerful material cards such as the Wheel of Fortune and the Devil are next to it. If the Fool comes before the Hermit, a secret will be safe, but if it comes after, a secret will be revealed. With the Chariot beside it, there will be sudden important news. If the Fool is next to the Sun, an unexpected triumph will bring comfort, order, and joy.

1 THE MAGICIAN

The commencement card.

This card denotes the beginning of an important new life cycle, new opportunities to use communicative talents, new skills, willpower turning thought into action, success through initiative, adaptability, versatility, and self-confidence. It can also warn of guile and trickery, or the combination of personal and divine power used deviously and for selfish reasons.

Combinations The Magician next to the High Priestess symbolizes power used wrongly. If the Devil is next to the Magician, the two cards cancel each other out; if they appear opposite each other in the fifth and tenth positions of the Celtic Cross, an event will be canceled. If the Wheel of Fortune and the Magician are opposite each other in the fifth and tenth positions, there will be a delay.

2 THE HIGH PRIESTESS

The inner life.

Intuition, inner perception, esoteric knowledge, spiritual strength and protection, artistic and creative abilities, and a thirst for learning. This card often denotes a teacher.

Combinations When the High Priestess is upright and next to the Wheel of Fortune, there will be a victory and recompense in a legal matter; if the Priestess is reversed next to the Wheel of Fortune, it signifies a sudden upheaval and insecurity. If the Priestess is reversed before Temperance, a problem seems insurmountable.

3 THE EMPRESS

Natural, emotional, and material abundance.

Femininity, creative and physical growth, intuitive emotion, protective love, a happy and possibly wealthy marriage, domestic stability, mother love, children, wealth, harmony, abundance, good health after illness, a natural course of events that proves beneficial, and a kind benefactor.

Combinations Followed by the Chariot, the Empress signifies an important financial increase. When followed by the Magician, diplomacy will bring success in a difficult situation. If the Empress is next to the Devil, the Tower, or Death—the strongly physical cards of the Major Arcana—both cards are canceled out.

4 THE EMPEROR

The dominating male force.

A governing force, logical thought, analysis, wealth and power of the temporal kind, self-discipline, stability, leadership, passion and romance, creative energy, intellectual power and activity, intelligence dominating passion, and knowledge gained through experience.

Combinations When surrounded by cards from the suit of Pentacles, it denotes that an important, responsible, but onerous position connected with finance will be offered. When followed by the World, there will be a transient peace, usually on a national level.
If reversed in the same position, it signifies a personal conflict and loss of worldly power and position.

5 THE HIEROPHANT

Inspirational genius in the performing arts.

Traditional teaching, scientific and religious vocation, spirituality, established religions, desire for social approval, conventional behavior and beliefs, self-honesty, secrets revealed, and inspiration bringing success for those connected with the performing arts.

Combinations The Emperor and the Hierophant together represent a struggle between spiritual and materialistic desires. The Hierophant coming first signifies that pride will cause a financial loss or the failure of an enterprise. If the Emperor comes first, power and position will be lost through lack of learning.

6 THE LOVERS

Difficult trial or choice between love and desire.

Love and marriage, a moral choice that depends upon the integrity of the querent, a choice between love and physical attraction or between love and career, success after an emotional trial, an intuitive decision, harmony, affection, and friendship. When negatively aspected, it indicates the envy and interference of others.

Combinations The Chariot before the Lovers signifies a sudden departure that will end a project or romance. The Chariot after the Lovers means a sudden, shocking discovery of a betrayal. The Magician following the Lovers symbolizes delay and indecision about a new venture or artistic work, and if the Lovers is reversed, hesitation will bring separation.

7 THE CHARIOT

Balancing positive and negative forces.

Sustained effort at solving stressful problems with patience and endurance will result in triumph, success, wealth, and prestige, often for those engaged in artistic pursuits. The Chariot also denotes sudden news, fast luxurious travel, and triumph over enemies.

Combinations Coming before the Tower, the Chariot means sustained effort brings success. When before the Hierophant, it denotes a relative triumph, and before the World, ambitions realized. If it comes before the Moon, a secret that has been hidden comes to light, and when it follows the Moon, it signifies a sickness or illness. If the Moon is reversed, the scandal or illness will not be severe.

8 JUSTICE

Balanced judgment and control.

A well-balanced outlook, a balance of mind and personality, a favorable outcome in legal or educational matters, honesty, integrity, the voice of inner conscience, or the vindication of truth and integrity, depending on the moral position of the querent.

Combinations When this card comes before the Hanged Man, it means tolerance is needed rather than harsh judgment. If followed by the High Priestess, a legal secret may be revealed, and if coming after the High Priestess, the same secret is revealed only through legal methods. If both cards are reversed, legal events miscarry or justice fails.

9 THE HERMIT

Guided by inner light and spiritual strength.

Thought and planning needed to make progress on a necessary but unfamiliar path, delayed attainment, silent counsel, wisdom from above, a beneficial meeting with a wise person, a journey bringing enlightenment, and sudden insight.

Combinations The Hermit coming before the Devil signifies that dangerous matters and devious enemies will be revealed and overcome by the Hermit's light. However, if the Devil precedes the Hermit, it means the Devil's power is stronger. If followed by the High Priestess, a secret matter will never be discovered, but if the High Priestess comes before the Hermit, patient investigation will reveal a long-held secret.

10 THE WHEEL OF FORTUNE

You reap what you sow.

This card symbolizes karma, or the law of retribution. It signifies a sudden change, usually resulting from past efforts, that can cause difficulties or setbacks but generally brings success or material wealth, wisdom gained from experience, a creative breakthrough, and events that will solve a problem.

Combinations Next to the Chariot, it means a great triumph. Next to the Hermit, it signifies that secrets revealed will bring success. If it comes before the High Priestess, there will be success in the arts, literature, or science. When the Magician precedes it, there will be a happy change in profession, direction, or dwelling, but if the Magician comes after it, the change will take longer to occur. When next to the Magician, High Priestess, or World, it means lasting success and good fortune.

11 STRENGTH

The triumph of positive forces over negative.

The strongest and most positive card in the tarot, it denotes strength of character, the triumph of love over hate, mastery of life and circumstances, self-discipline, endurance, mind over matter, and a once-in-a-lifetime opportunity that must be taken.

Combinations Strength influences every other card in a reading and helps to lessen the impact of negative cards. If before Death, it means recovery after a serious illness, and after Death, a sudden transformation of a way of life. If it precedes the Chariot, it denotes that sustained work will bring triumph, and after the Chariot, it promises great strength in facing future problems and trials.

12 THE HANGED MAN

A willing sacrifice entailing hardship.

Depending on the surrounding cards, the Hanged Man can denote inner strength, occult power, and a spiritual decision that brings hardship. It can also signify either serenity, wisdom, forgiveness, and spiritual peace, or renunciation, destruction, and abandonment—both will transform or reverse a way of life.

Combinations If the Devil comes before the Hanged Man, a marriage partner will make a sacrifice to ensure contentment, but the other partner must be prepared to give more. If the Devil comes after, a great sacrifice will bring strength and power. With Death next to it, it means a sad ending, and when Temperance is beside it, false promises that cause hypocrisy or indecision.

13 DEATH

Death of the old life brings rebirth of the soul.

A deeply spiritual card, Death denotes a change in consciousness, destruction, transformation, regeneration of the soul, the end of an unbearable situation, and an artistic or creative struggle that ends in triumph.

Combinations Death covers both personal and national disasters. Coming after the Lovers, it means the end of a marriage or romance, and when beside the Tower, it can denote a calamity or a crisis. If it appears before the World, there will be either a world disaster, a universal epidemic, or the loss of a world leader.

14 TEMPERANCE

Moderation and balance.

A balanced attitude to life, an even temperament, the combination of the spiritual and material, moderation, compromise, successful combinations, stalemate before synthesis, future peace and harmony, success in financial management, creative inspiration, and energy and vitality.

Combinations When the Lovers is next to Temperance, it means indecision, but if the Lovers is reversed, it indicates that a lover is deceitful. When Justice comes after Temperance, a long legal process will bring justice, but if Justice comes first, there will be delays and even cancellation. However, if Temperance is reversed in either position, delays will end and there will be success.

15 THE DEVIL

Power and physical appetites used negatively.

This is the most negative card in the deck and means a strong force fueled by ignorance, greed, or fear, superstition used unwisely, physical domination, carnal desire, lack of sensitivity, materialism, illness, and wealth obtained dishonestly. It also indicates a sudden inexorable event, either positive or negative, depending on surrounding cards.

Combinations If next to the Hierophant, the meaning of both cards is canceled and the other cards in the spread will show the outcome. If followed by Justice, there will be a miscarriage of justice, but if Justice comes first, it will be proved to be a false accusation. When the Devil comes before the powerful Emperor, it means a national protest, but if the Emperor precedes the Devil, a world leader will be attacked or threatened with violence.

16 THE TOWER

Disruption bringing eventual happiness.

A sudden change of life's pattern, an unexpected shock or catastrophe, selfish ambitions or illusions shattered, a cleansing catharsis, traditions challenged, a flash of inspiration, and the beginning of enlightenment.

Combinations Coming before the High Priestess, it can mean a disaster either in traditional institutions or in a religious sphere, but if these two cards are reversed, it denotes that a mental breakdown followed by a physical collapse could be imminent. If the World is near these two cards, the meaning is more general than personal.

17 THE STAR

Hope, love, encouragement, and rebirth.

This card symbolizes spiritual guidance and unselfish love. It can indicate that help and encouragement from friends will bring refreshment of mind and spirit after a period of darkness, or that optimism will bring about a rebirth that results in spiritual inspiration and renewed effort.

Combinations If the Devil appears next to the Star, they cancel each other out and other cards in the spread will show the outcome. If the Star comes after the Empress, there will be a happy, peaceful, and conventional life. If the Empress comes first, sustained effort linked with strong ambition brings assured success. If the Magician comes after the Star, it denotes the fortunate beginning of a business project or an artistic venture.

18 THE MOON

The subconscious, imagination, and illusion.

The subconscious, hidden forces, deception, illusion, mystery, dreams, creativity, fluctuation, uncertainty, emotional crisis, storms weathered, or a loved one's misfortune or illness.

Combinations The Moon followed by the Lovers indicates false love, an illusion of love, or deception and lies that ruin a relationship. Coming before the Tower, the Moon can mean self-deception, deceit, or fraud bringing misfortune. When it appears before Justice, it denotes false accusations or slander. When both cards are reversed, the truth will be discovered.

19 THE SUN

Success, happiness, purity, strength, and courage.

A positive card denoting triumphant achievements in any field against all odds, studies completed, ambitions realized, protection, harmonious meetings and relationships, material happiness, health, energy, the gift of gratitude, and the end of self-deception.

Combinations When next to the Two of Cups, it symbolizes two positive and loving people creating a permanent relationship. If Death follows the Sun, it means a triumphant end to something. When followed by the Tower, a sudden shock or catastrophe will eventually bring great benefit.

20 JUDGMENT

A new lease on life or a reincarnation.

A powerful, highly spiritual card, Judgment denotes the end of one period in life and the beginning of another, change and renewal, rewards for past efforts, pride in achievements, a life well spent, and a mental awakening that could precede fame and success.

Combinations When Judgment is followed by the Chariot, it means triumphant success and fame, but if the Chariot is reversed, the triumph may only be temporary because sudden success could weaken the character. Followed by the Hermit, there will be inner spiritual triumph.

21 THE WORLD

The reward for well-learned lessons.

This is the wish card of the Major Arcana and denotes the seeker of perfection who attains great success and both material and spiritual rewards. It also symbolizes a triumphant conclusion or the end of a cycle of life, joy, happiness, dreams coming true, and long-distance travel across water.

Combinations The spirituality of this card is canceled by the proximity of the Magician, the Hermit, or Justice. Next to the Sun, it represents an emotional experience that brings love, joy, and harmony. The Hanged Man coming after the World means a loving sacrifice brings happiness and triumph, but if the World comes first, a sacrifice could lead to a sad parting.

The Minor Arcana

The Minor Arcana consists of 56 cards divided into four suits: Cups (also known as Chalices); Pentacles (also called Deniers); Wands (sometimes known as Staves, Batons, or Clubs); and Swords. Each suit has 14 cards: ace to ten, and four court cards—knave, knight, queen, and king. Although less significant than the Major Arcana, these cards add clarity to a reading and give more depth to the spiritual and emotional concerns of the querent.

THE SUIT OF CUPS

Cups are connected with the element water. The changeable nature of water represents the emotions, and water's hidden depths symbolize the subconscious. The suit of Cups therefore denotes the emotions of love and pleasure, and the subconscious mind and instincts. When these cards appear in a spread they indicate joy, love, human relationships, friendship, home, fulfillment, procreation, family ties, and obligations. Although they do have a spiritual connection, they are mainly concerned with worldly happiness and physical pleasure. Cups are generally positive cards, but if negatively aspected, they can indicate jealousy and excessive emotion.

THE SUIT OF WANDS

Wands are linked with fire, symbolizing strength, growth, and the power of renewal. This suit is connected with work of all kinds and the spark of creative imagination. The cards denote lasting values such as emotional and material security, talent, artistic endeavors, expansion, and stability. Fire is a catalyst, so the suit of Wands signifies all types of activity, from creative imagination to career and inner development. Wands also represent strength in adversity, and indicate that hard work and prolonged effort will bring success and security. When negatively aspected, the suit can also symbolize laziness and lack of integrity.

THE SUIT OF PENTACLES

Pentacles represent the element earth and all aspects of material existence. The suit is strongly connected with money and denotes all types of financial transaction, material gain, windfalls, inheritance, and legal matters concerning finance. When Pentacles appear in a spread, they often indicate that wealthy and powerful people will provide help to the querent, which will lead to fulfillment in career and finances. When negatively aspected, however, they can signify unemployment, poverty, too great a reliance on money, and misuse of wealth.

THE SUIT OF SWORDS

Swords are linked with air and therefore symbolize abstract thought and mental and spiritual development. This is the strongest suit of the Minor Arcana and denotes conflict, spiritual strength, loss and partings, sadness, worry, trials, competition, and loneliness of spirit. The sword is also a symbol of physical aggression and can denote sacrifice, loss, and defeat. This suit is therefore often seen as primarily negative. However, although it does stand for struggle and hardship, it also carries the message that if those struggles are faced with courage, they will eventually lead to spiritual enlightenment, maturity, peace, and success.

The Suit of Cups

ACE OF CUPS

The feminine gestation card.

The Ace of Cups denotes creative inspiration, faith, spiritual nourishment, good news, bright company, a new romantic meeting, and great rewards from a loving union. When near other love cards, it means true love and perhaps marriage. If near the Empress, it signifies motherhood and fruitful abundance.

TWO OF CUPS

Emotion and spirituality create a permanent bond.

A deep understanding of another person results in a loving union, a love affair, an engagement, or a lasting friendship. It also signifies a new partnership, a contract or agreement signed, the reconciliation of opposites, or reconciliation after a parting, the end of rivalry or quarrels, a happy surprise, or limited money and support given.

THREE OF CUPS

Emotional growth and fulfillment in relationships.

The feminine element in nature brings emotional growth, happiness, and fulfillment in all relationships. Sensitivity and generosity to others lead to lifelong love and friendship. Creative ability brings happiness, congratulations, and reward, wounds are healed, and there will be a victorious conclusion to a matter.

FOUR OF CUPS

The divine discontent card.

A re-evaluation of life and material success leads to new paths and directions being taken. The querent should listen to his or her inner voice in matters of the heart when hostility from jealous people threatens to ruin a future romance or friendship.

FIVE OF CUPS

Something ended, a new beginning.

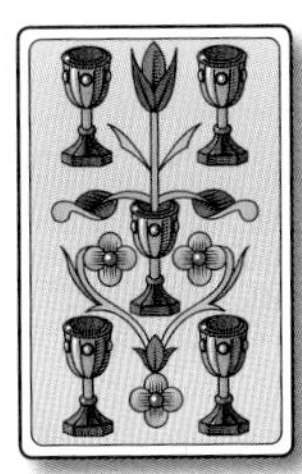

After regretting a wrong choice, a mistake, past actions, or the loss of a marriage partner or friend, new paths lie ahead as long as spiritual needs are never ignored. If positively aspected, it can also mean inheritance or gifts.

SIX OF CUPS

Past efforts bring present rewards.

This is the card of conflict and reconciliation. The results of past actions or contacts now bring benefits, something is beginning that has its roots in the past, or an old friend, lover, or long-held dream comes to fruition. When negatively aspected, it carries a warning not to live in the past.

SEVEN OF CUPS

Imagination, dreams, and mystical experiences.

Creative inspiration, mental activity, a surprise connected with mental or creative activity, or an unexpected and exceptional choice that will need care, consideration, and wisdom to fulfill a dream. There is a warning that the querent could become "Jack of all trades, master of none."

EIGHT OF CUPS

Refined by the flame to rise like a phoenix.

Maturity through suffering, a new path in life after leaving the past behind or abandoning a place or situation, genuine artistic and spiritual friends, and new activities that bring joy and fulfillment.

NINE OF CUPS

The strong and positive wish card.

Success, good luck, good health, generosity, kindness, emotional and material stability, intuitive awareness, and the total fulfillment of one major wish or desire. There is a warning that overindulgence and contentment in life's pleasures will undermine artistic efforts and commitments.

TEN OF CUPS

Work to do with the public brings success and prosperity.

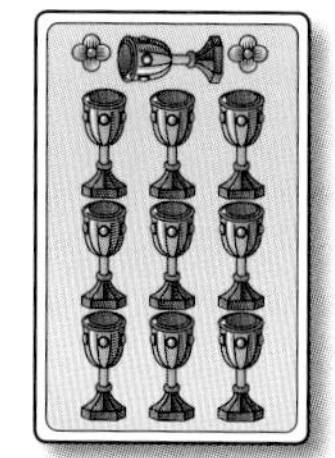

Legal and financial matters concerned with family, property, or residence, prosperity, peace of mind, loving friends, work to do with the public, publicity, prestige, fame, honor, and lasting success.

KNAVE OF CUPS

A change that improves the future.

A quiet, meditative artistic youth of either sex, under 21, who is willing, helpful, but sometimes deceptive through being overly imaginative or overemotional. It also means the birth of a child, new business methods, a change that improves the future, and a message or news.

KNIGHT OF CUPS

A fated relationship that teaches a lesson.

A man between 21 and 35, intelligent, highly principled except possibly in emotional matters, romantic, sometimes egotistical and devious, a friend, lover, seducer, or a rival in love, also the bearer of a message, an invitation, a proposition, a pleasant visit, or a fated relationship.

QUEEN OF CUPS

A loving idealist practicing what she preaches.

A loved one or mistress over the age of 21, romantic, highly artistic, slightly fey, intuitive, prophetic, a visionary, sensitive, a good mixer, idealistic, new romance, or new horizons. Negatively aspected, it signifies moodiness, self-deception, overdominance, or false romanticism.

KING OF CUPS

A professional man gives help and good advice.

A man over 35 from any walk of life, usually a professional in the fields of law, education, medicine, or religion. Mentally strong, skilled in the ways of the world, warm-hearted, sympathetic, sensitive, creative, but hides emotion. A man of ideas, he could make a good romantic partner but can often be crafty and put himself first.

The Suit of Wands

ACE OF WANDS

A new foundation for success.

New beginnings, new undertakings, and dissatisfaction with present circumstances. Innovation or artistic inspiration brings a new cycle of creative activity, a new foundation results in satisfaction and success, new wisdom, new knowledge, or the founding of a family or fortune.

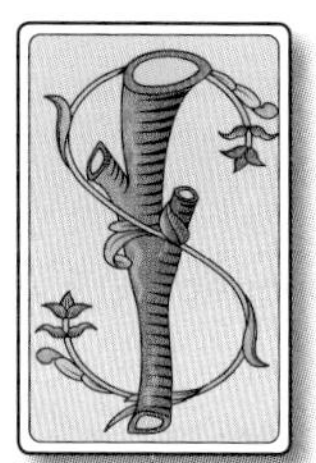

TWO OF WANDS

Success won through strength and vision.

Intellectual activity, tolerance, justice, high motives, high principles, consistent effort. Initiation and courage overcoming obstacles bring maturity, future happiness, and success. Help from a scientific authority.

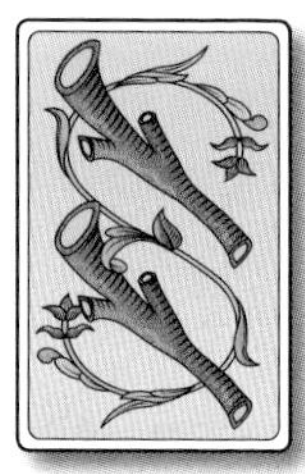

THREE OF WANDS

Artist or inventor who turns dreams into reality.

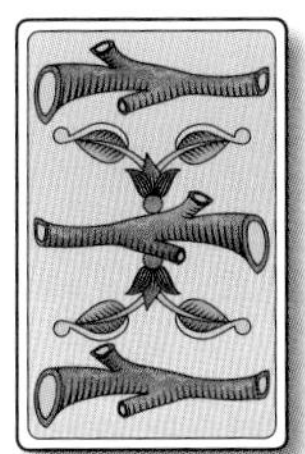

With original ideas, powerful convictions, and fine powers of expression, inspirational work brings reward and recognition to the artist or inventor. Also denotes a successful business enterprise or partnership, help from a powerful friend, but warns against carelessness.

FOUR OF WANDS

Good harvest and happy home.

Successful designer or inventor, the combination of professional ideas with perfected work, a peaceful period away from the demands of society or a pause in activities, close family ties, romance, harmony, and the gathering of the harvest after long hard labor.

FIVE OF WANDS

A struggle in love and in life ends in success.

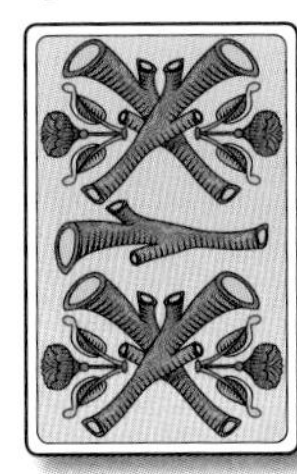

Love triumphs over obstacles or a determined struggle overcomes material adversity and brings a change for the better, with the warning that mental ability is needed to succeed. Badly aspected, it means carelessness in legal matters or bitterness through unfulfilled desires.

SIX OF WANDS

The career card.

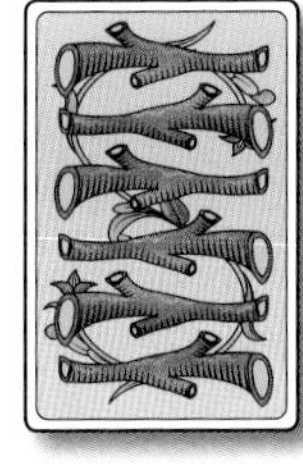

The fulfillment of ambition, a triumphant achievement in career, the solution to a major problem, victory in a difficult situation, diplomacy conquers opposition, success after a struggle, great satisfaction through achievement, and wonderful news. There is also a warning that the envy of others could sour triumph.

SEVEN OF WANDS

The teacher's card.

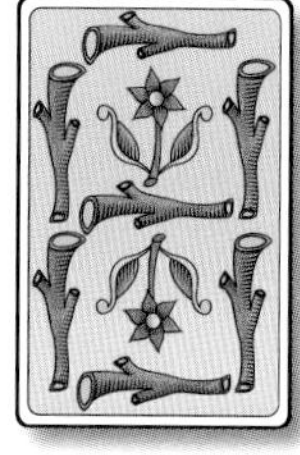

Lecturing, writing, and the dissemination of knowledge, a successful professional change, inner strength and determination help to achieve success, and opposition defeated by courage and sustained effort. Badly aspected, it denotes envy from others, failure from indecision, or a need for competitiveness.

EIGHT OF WANDS

Movement and speed or the sudden arrows of love.

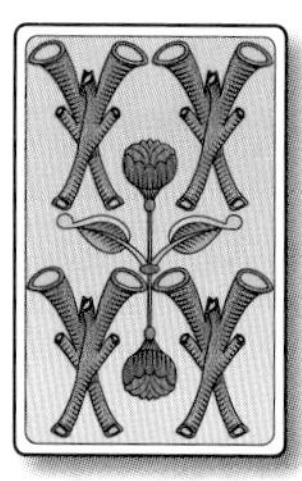

A time to be active and doing something new, sudden changes that bring progress, sudden unexpected news, a sudden journey, speed, hasty travel by air, overseas connections, the end of a period of calm or delay, and new love.

NINE OF WANDS

The strongest card in the Minor Arcana.

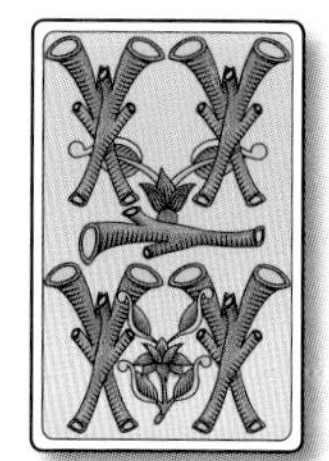

A final challenge met with strength and integrity brings victory and a lasting triumph. A safe and unassailable position, success in artistic or professional fields, expansion, honesty, balanced judgment, courage in defense, strength in reserve, and a trusting nature.

TEN OF WANDS

Burdens soon to be lifted.

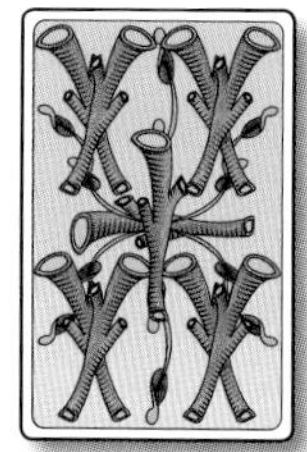

Burdens lifted, problems solved, narrow-minded ideas must go before progressing in a new direction, new contracts, new ventures, consolidation, big business, or an overseas journey to a strange place. Badly aspected, it indicates fear of risk or an unrealistic opinion of abilities.

KNAVE OF WANDS

Creative potential and lack of direction.

A youth of either sex under 21 who has a talent that needs developing or who lacks direction in life. A messenger, a letter with happy news from a loved one, or stimulating information about finances. When next to another court card, it symbolizes honors or good news concerning a youth or child.

KNIGHT OF WANDS

The intuition card and the traveler or immigrant.

A charming, lovable, volatile, and intuitive man over 21 and under 35, who loves change, particularly travel, and who has a stable sense in money matters. It also denotes distant travel, flight or departure, or a change of residence.

QUEEN OF WANDS

The home and country lover.

An intuitive, generous, tolerant, protective, strong-willed, confident, independent, creative, and artistic woman over the age of 21 who loves country life and home. The card could represent a good friend or success in a new business or creative venture. Badly aspected, she is dominant, judgmental, and bitter.

KING OF WANDS

A born leader.

A man over 35, honest, intelligent, courageous, generous, and enthusiastic, giving wise, sympathetic, and impartial advice, and achieving success in a financial, creative, or professional field. Also denotes an unexpected inheritance. Badly aspected, he could be power-hungry.

The Suit of Pentacles

ACE OF PENTACLES

Security based on a firm foundation.

Love of possessions, materialism, prosperity, gold, legacies, luxury, gifts, security, stoicism, endurance, pride in one's own success, love of physical beauty, sensuousness, and a new enterprise bringing sound financial benefit. Badly aspected, it can mean greed or overconfidence.

TWO OF PENTACLES

Skillful manipulation brings successful change.

Fluctuation in fortune, imminent change, skillful manipulation bringing harmony despite sudden domestic or financial change, literary ability, one talent bringing rewards, and a journey to a new home or country. Negatively aspected, emotional instability could cause problems.

THREE OF PENTACLES

Professionalism and craftsmanship.

Training, learning, and consistent effort bring skill in a trade or artistic ability resulting in success, recognition, honor, esteem, and financial rewards. Also symbolizes cooperation or help from others or a good time for business expansion. Negatively aspected, it denotes loss through lack of direction.

FOUR OF PENTACLES

Benefit and loss in financial matters.

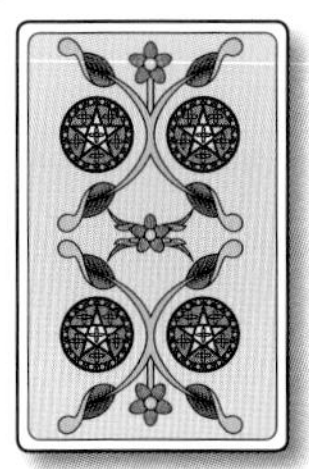

Material and financial stability, acquisitiveness, love of possessions, financial obstacles and problems, a legacy or inheritance, and the establishment of a commercial firm or business. Negatively aspected, it indicates miserliness, low self-esteem, and commercial and financial problems.

FIVE OF PENTACLES

Allowing the heart to rule the head brings trouble.

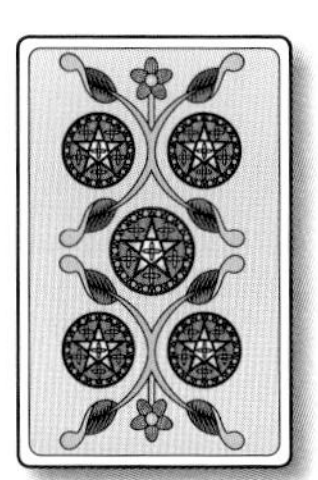

Loss of judgment, work, lover, or home, sorrow, disappointment, spiritual loneliness, or enforced restrictions. However, lasting friendships will be made with those in similar circumstances, and when positively aspected, it can mean that faith in oneself is regained and a new start made.

SIX OF PENTACLES

The theatrical and entertainment card.

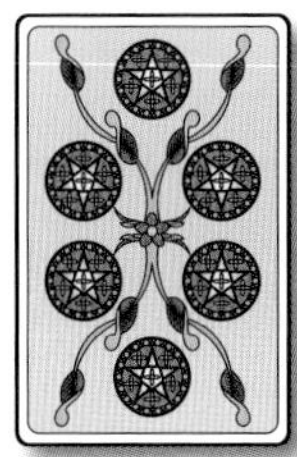

A strongly spiritual card, it means help from above or from a generous and good person, charity, kindness, sympathy, just rewards, and stable finances. It also denotes acting, singing, dancing, and lecturing. If negatively aspected, it means the inability to give of oneself.

SEVEN OF PENTACLES

Procrastination is the thief of time.

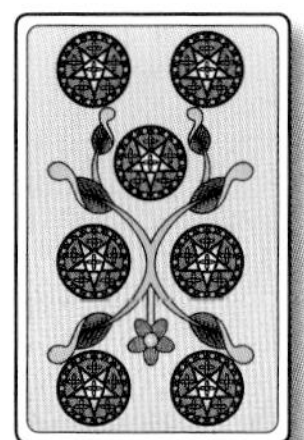

A gift or sudden gain, new love, money though barter or a loan, something changing, or results from the past about to bear fruit. It also warns against delay, saying consistent work is needed to make past efforts a complete success.

EIGHT OF PENTACLES

The talent and energy card.

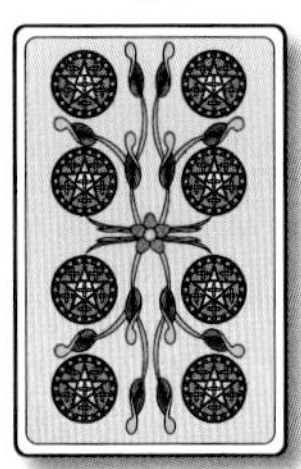

A change bringing material benefits, a recently discovered skill turned into a profession, future employment and success from developing a talent or skill, work rewarded, or work beginning again. Negatively aspected, it warns of failure through laziness.

NINE OF PENTACLES

Self-knowledge brings inner peace.

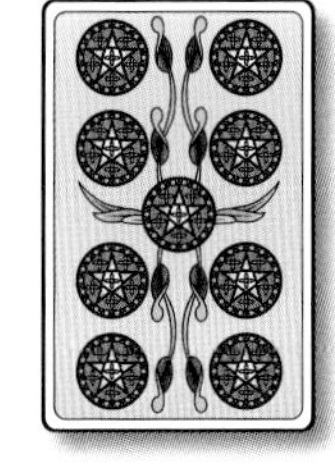

An independent, uniquely talented person must learn that self-knowledge brings peace and happiness. It also signifies material wealth, good income earned by consistent effort and sound administration, a successful completion bringing reward and comfort, or the solution to a problem.

TEN OF PENTACLES

The hearth, home, and family.

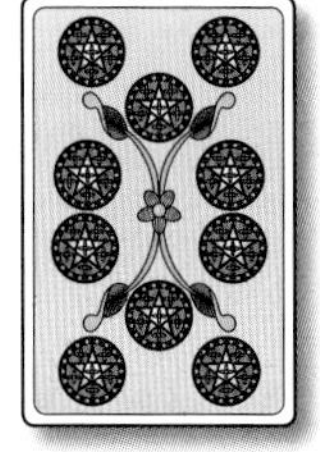

This card can mean rewards from creative achievements, spiritual, creative, and material wealth shared with others, but pertains more to family ties, inheritance, a settled life, homes bought or sold, reverence for history, or establishing traditions. Badly aspected, it signifies that restrictive ties can be a burden.

KNAVE OF PENTACLES

Respect for learning, new ideas, and opinions.

A person under 21 of either sex, diligent, ambitious, and respectful of new ideas, new opinions, learning, and scholarship, but who can also be miserly and materialistic. Also denotes a message with good news or a letter containing money. If badly aspected, it symbolizes unrealistic aims, intellectual snobbery, and wasted talent.

QUEEN OF PENTACLES

Responsibility with wealth.

An independent, industrious, practical woman over 21, sometimes financially secure, socially adept, and interested in the creative arts, who loves the good things in life, has a sense of responsibility toward those not as well off, and gives generously to those she respects. Badly aspected, she can be insecure, materialistic, or cynical.

KNIGHT OF PENTACLES

Patience needed to finish laborious work.

A man between 21 and 35, a nature and animal lover, honorable, traditional, determined, and materialistic, a new acquaintance, an indiscreet flirtation, the beginning and end of a matter, or patience needed to finish hard and laborious work. Badly aspected, mistakes can be made through timidity or stagnation.

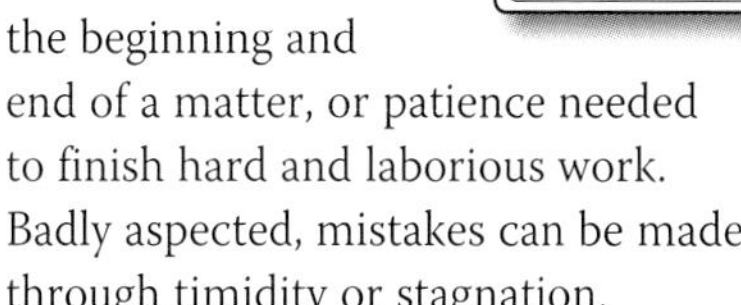

KING OF PENTACLES

Mathematical skill in financial matters.

A man over 35, stable, inarticulate, intuitive, wise, patient, loyal to friends, often uneducated with a deliberate turn of mind and a flair for mathematics, and may be connected with financial matters. He is a good parent but a bad enemy, and badly aspected, is easy to bribe.

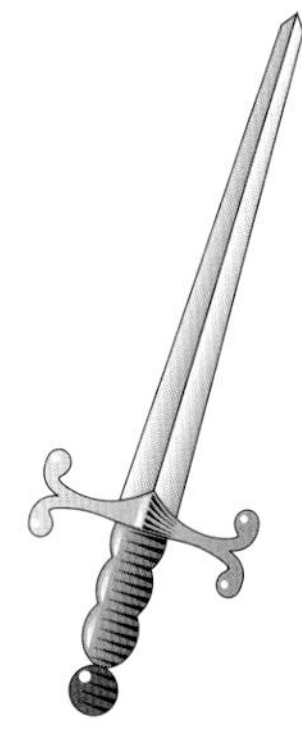

THE SUIT OF SWORDS

ACE OF SWORDS

Divine justice, or you reap what you sow.

Conquest, just rewards, a sense of the inevitable, something that cannot be stopped that changes the querent's perspective on life, a strong force for good or ill, and strength in adversity. Negatively aspected, it means victory and lessons learned after disappointment.

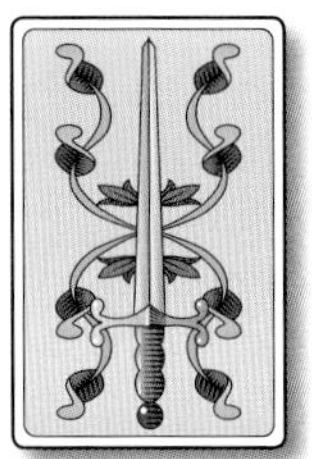

TWO OF SWORDS

Balanced forces or stalemate.

A sense of equilibrium, good coming out of evil, help and friendship in adversity, or a difficult choice that results in spiritual peace and inner satisfaction. Negatively aspected, it denotes a wrong choice as a result of indecision, self-deception, and living in the past.

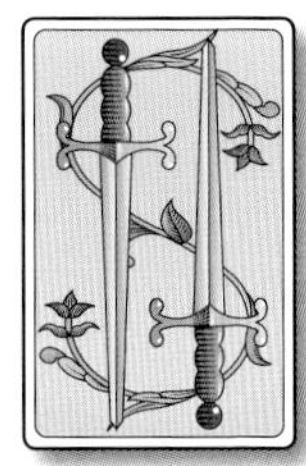

THREE OF SWORDS

The darkest hour before the dawn.

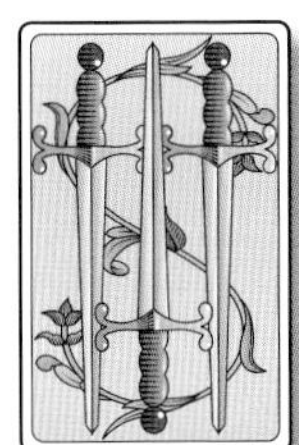

Disruption, upheaval, ties severed, tears over a faithless lover, marital break-up, partnership severed, and permanent or temporary separation. If positively aspected, it signifies pain followed by healing and clearing the ground for something new. Negatively aspected, it means civil strife or dwelling on old hurts.

FOUR OF SWORDS

Peace and order after struggle and chaos.

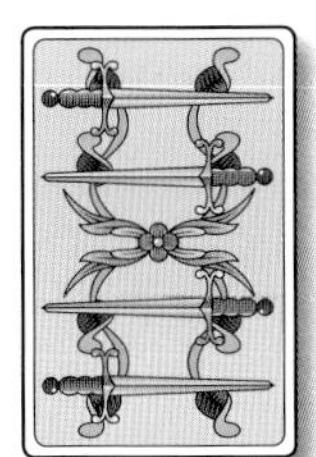

A voluntary retreat after a testing time to think things through, rest, hospitalization, convalescence, occultism, religion, meditation, or legal administration in a personal or civic sense after struggle and chaos. Negatively aspected, it means diplomacy needed, a decision postponed, or a feeling of isolation.

FIVE OF SWORDS

Accept limitations to move onward and upward.

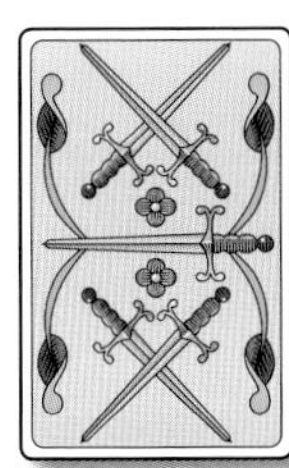

Accept the inevitable with courage, acknowledge defeat, and recognize and swallow false pride in order to build on secure foundations and proceed in a new direction. Also symbolizes a threat averted or a narrow escape from danger. Negatively aspected, it means fear and insecurity bring a humiliating defeat.

SIX OF SWORDS

Flight or travel, and risk bringing reward.

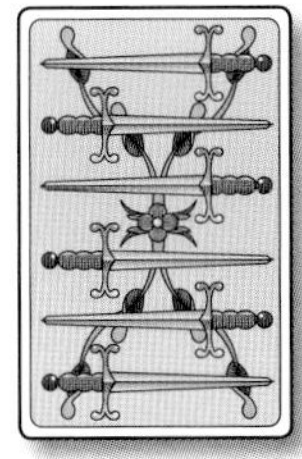

Travel, flight, a change to a better environment or a better position, a large obstacle removed after time of stress, success after a difficult time, or good news brought by an overseas visitor. Negatively aspected, it warns the querent to be patient—time will solve a problem.

SEVEN OF SWORDS

Use brain not brawn to achieve success.

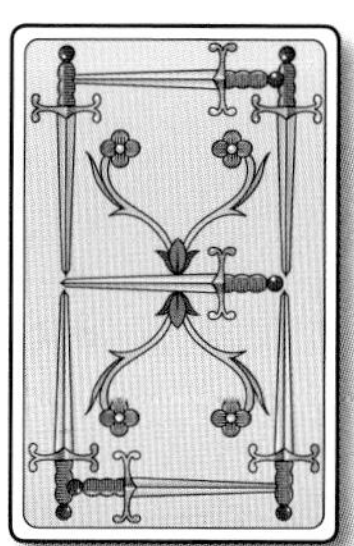

Prudence, evasion, foresight, and cunning are all needed to solve a problem, thwart an enemy, sidestep an obstacle, and gain an objective. Aggression will bring disaster. Negatively aspected, it indicates partial success, uncertain hope, altered plans, danger of injury in travel or sport, and dwelling on mistakes that will block progress.

EIGHT OF SWORDS

Restrictions will soon be lifted.

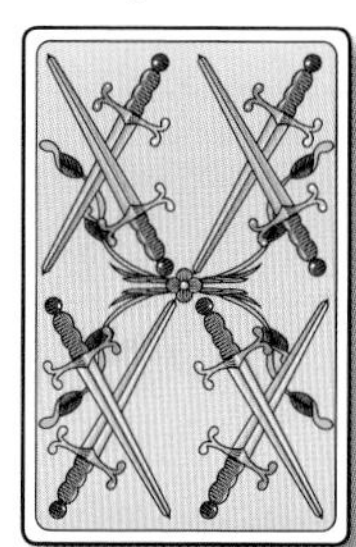

Bonds will soon be broken, but self-honesty, confidence, patience, and attention to detail are needed to bring about change and avoid criticism. As hurts heal, a new self-confidence brings progress, but lack of confidence, self-deception, hypocrisy, or negativity can all cause indecision.

NINE OF SWORDS

Time heals all wounds.

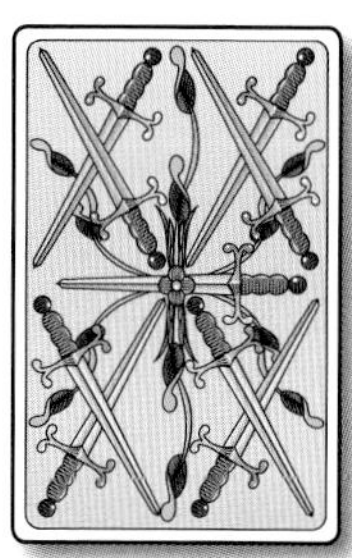

A difficult choice entailing sacrifice, patient suffering borne with fortitude and courage, illness, loss, isolation, news of a road accident or death, or a sense of despair or self-punishment. Favorably aspected, it means shedding the past and beginning a new and productive life.

TEN OF SWORDS

See things as they are, not what they appear to be.

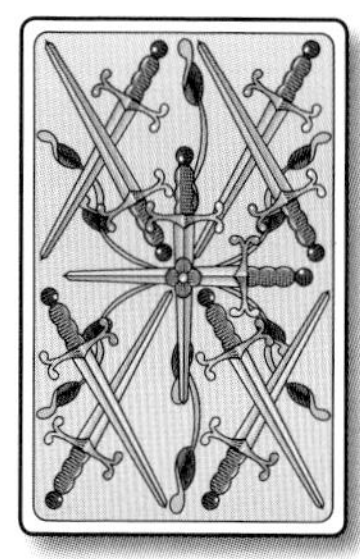

The lowest ebb in both human affairs and the national economy, bringing self-honesty that now sees something clearly for what it really is. Negatively aspected, it can mean pain and sudden misfortune, but when favorably aspected, it denotes the end of spiritual darkness, new self-acceptance, and a rebirth.

KNAVE OF SWORDS

Inner conflict creates problems.

An independent young person under 21 of either sex who possibly suffered injustice in childhood and whose inner conflict makes him or her frivolous, mischievous, unpredictable, manipulative, devious, and cruel. Also signifies a diplomatic or foreign messenger who negotiates business, an unscrupulous business rival, a deceitful person carrying tales, or a spy.

KNIGHT OF SWORDS

A man who enters the querent's life for good or ill.

A strong, passionate, career-minded man over 21 and under 35, who is an impetuous, courageous, and sometimes ruthless fighter. He is at his best in a difficult situation. The card can also signify a struggle yet to come, a conflict to be faced, or a foreign man or nation. When near cards denoting illness, it represents a surgeon.

QUEEN OF SWORDS

The widow's card.

A woman over 21, possibly a widow carrying a sense of sadness and privation with her, who is strong, intelligent, self-reliant, cautious, and makes a good friend but an intolerant and spiteful enemy. Also represents a struggle between material and spiritual values, attention to detail, and a foreign woman or nation.

KING OF SWORDS

An authoritative, innovative intellectual.

An authoritative man over 35, a professional or an intellectual with moral convictions and an innovative mind, he could be a lawyer, an adviser, a counselor, a high government official, or an officer in the armed forces. He also denotes a foreign man or nation, and when badly aspected, is a severe critic who can be violent, cruel, and vengeful.

INDEX

A

activities 79
aspect, positive/negative 27, 32
atmosphere, creating 24, 28

B

Bohemian Spread 34-80
  answers 40-45, 50-55, 60-65, 70-75
  choosing cards 18
  evaluating cards 19
  full reading 76-80
  questions 36-39, 46-49, 56-59, 66-69

C

cards
  choice of 24, 28
  looking after 24, 28
  meanings 187-217
    learning 27, 32
  positively/negatively aspected 27, 31
  reversed 27, 31
career
  and current influences 66-75
  and luck 56-65
  and success 94-103
Celtic Cross 130-185
  answers 136-139, 144-148, 154-158, 164-169, 174-180
  choosing cards 23
  evaluating cards 23
  final outcome 150-158, 170-180
  full reading 182-185
  Major Arcana 132-158
  Minor Arcana 160-180
  questions 132-135, 140-143, 150-153, 160-163, 170-173
character, personal 116-125
Chariot 192
  Bohemian Spread 39, 45, 47, 49, 51, 53, 54, 56, 60, 69, 74, 75, 78
  Celtic Cross 133, 137, 141, 143, 145, 147, 151, 155, 171, 175
  Romany Draw 113, 127
couples, readings for 24, 30
Cups 200, 202-205
  Ace 202
    Bohemian Spread 37, 42, 47, 51
    Celtic Cross 161, 165
    Romany Draw 89
  Two 202

Bohemian Spread 37, 38, 41, 42-43, 47, 52
Romany Draw 93, 103, 122
Three 203
Bohemian Spread 38, 43
Romany Draw 91, 108
Four 203
Bohemian Spread 47, 51, 79
Celtic Cross 163, 168
Five 203
Bohemian Spread 58, 63
Celtic Cross 162, 166, 183
Romany Draw 592, 102, 114, 121
Six 203
Bohemian Spread 36, 40
Celtic Cross 185
Romany Draw 92, 114
Seven 204
Bohemian Spread 48, 53
Celtic Cross 171, 175
Romany Draw 122
Eight 204
Bohemian Spread 49, 55
Romany Draw 125
Nine 204
Bohemian Spread 38, 43
Ten 204
Celtic Cross 173, 178
Romany Draw 90, 105
Knave 205
Bohemian Spread 37, 41
Knight 205
Bohemian Spread 38, 42, 57, 62
Romany Draw 89
Queen 205
Bohemian Spread 47, 49, 51, 54, 79
Celtic Cross 183
Romany Draw 93
King 205
Romany Draw 106, 122
representing querent 16

D

Death 195
Bohemian Spread 67, 71-72
Celtic Cross 133, 135, 137, 139, 141, 145, 170, 174
Romany Draw 98, 100
deck
choice of 24, 28
meanings 187-217
Delphic Oracle 8
desires 36-45, 76
Devil 196
Bohemian Spread 48, 54, 58, 62
Celtic Cross 132, 136, 142, 147, 172, 177, 184
Romany Draw 102, 113, 120, 124
domestic matters 78

E

Emperor 190
Bohemian Spread 58-63
Celtic Cross 134, 138, 142, 146, 163, 168, 171, 175
Romany Draw 122
Empress 190
Bohemian Spread 37, 41
Celtic Cross 133, 137, 143, 148
Romany Draw 92
ethics 8

F

family 185
  feelings and 140-148
  influences 77
feelings 140-148
  negative 184
Fool 188
  Bohemian Spread 59, 65
  Celtic Cross 151, 152, 155, 157, 173, 188
fortune 78
  career and 56-59
friends/friendship 40-45, 185
  feelings and 140-148
  full reading 76
  and unexpected 46-55

G

Greece, Ancient 8

H

Hanged Man 194
  Bohemian Spread 37, 39, 41, 45, 49, 55, 77
  Celtic Cross 134, 138, 139, 162, 163, 167, 169
  Romany Draw 105, 121
health 104-115
Hermit 193
  Bohemian Spread 39, 44, 59, 65
  Celtic Cross 134, 138, 185
  Romany Draw 103, 112
Hierophant 191
  Celtic Cross 143, 148, 152, 157, 184
  Romany Draw 102
High Priestess 189
  Bohemian Spread 67, 68, 71, 73
  Celtic Cross 133, 135, 137, 139, 151, 153, 160, 164
  Romany Draw 108, 124

I

influences 132-139
  and career 66-75
  full readings 77, 78, 183, 184

J

Judgment 198
  Celtic Cross 140, 141, 144, 145, 152, 156, 161, 166
  Romany Draw 98, 123
Justice 192
  Bohemian Spread 39, 45, 47, 52, 58, 63, 79
  Celtic Cross 134, 138, 151, 155
  Romany Draw 90

K

King, as significator 16
Knave, as significator 16
Knight, as significator 16

L

love
  and desires 36-45
  and romance 84-93
  and unexpected 46-55
Lovers 191

Bohemian Spread 38, 43, 49, 54, 57, 62, 69, 75
Celtic Cross 133, 137, 143, 148, 153, 157, 161, 165-166
luck 78
career and 56-65

M

Magician 189
Bohemian Spread 57, 59, 62, 64, 66, 68, 69, 70, 73, 75, 79
Celtic Cross 132, 136, 152
Romany Draw 48, 114, 123
Major Arcana
feelings 140-148
influences 132-139
meanings 188-199
with Minor Arcana 160-180
meanings 186-217
layers of 6
unclear 27, 32
meditation 17
Minor Arcana
answers 164-169, 174-180
meanings 200-217
questions 160-163, 170-173
Moon 197
Bohemian Spread 38, 44, 47, 48, 52, 69, 75
Celtic Cross 80, 81, 82, 83, 85, 87, 93, 97, 99, 103
Romany Draw 88, 98, 108, 112, 114

P

Pentacles 201, 210-213
Ace 210
Romany Draw 100, 122
Two 210
Bohemian Spread 68, 73, 76
Celtic Cross 173, 180
Romany Draw 105
Three 211
Bohemian Spread 39, 45, 56, 60, 79
Romany Draw 98-99
Four 211
Bohemian Spread 58, 62, 76
Romany Draw 101
Five 211
Bohemian Spread 48, 52, 58, 59, 63, 65
Celtic Cross 161, 166
Romany Draw 100, 105
Six 211
Seven 212
Bohemian Spread 46, 50
Romany Draw 103, 123
Eight 212
Bohemian Spread 69, 75, 78, 79
Celtic Cross 183
Romany Draw 103
Nine 212
Bohemian Spread 57, 61
Celtic Cross 173, 180
Ten 212
Celtic Cross 162, 168
Knave 213
Romany Draw 120
Knight 213
Bohemian Spread 38, 42-43
Queen 213
King 213
Bohemian Spread 68, 72

representing querent 16
personal character 116-125
predictions, apparently incorrect 27, 33
psychic powers 8
developing 24, 29

Q

Queen, as significator 16
querent 16
asking questions 24, 30
querying interpretation 27, 33
questions
asked by querent 24, 30
asked of querent 16
questions and answers 6

R

readings
conducting 16
for couples 24, 30
creating atmosphere 24, 28-29
ethics of 8-9
general questions 24, 27
answers 28-33
matters dealt with 8-9
personal interpretation 7
positive interpretation 9, 27, 31
querent querying 27, 33
theoretical 6
unclear meanings 27, 32
Rider-Waite deck 28
romance 36, 45, 84-93
full reading 79-80
and unexpected 46-55
Romany Draw 82-127
answers 88-93, 98-103, 108-115, 120-125
choosing cards 20
evaluating cards 21
full reading 126
questions 84-87, 94-97, 104-107, 116-119

S

self-fulfillment 9
self-knowledge 9
significator 16
sixth sense 8
spreads
see also Bohemian Spread; Celtic Cross; Romany Draw
designing 27, 31
selecting 17
Star 197
Bohemian Spread 46, 50, 66, 90-71
Celtic Cross 141, 145, 153, 158, 171, 176
Romany Draw 88-89, 106
Strength 194
Bohemian Spread 48, 53, 57, 61, 67, 72
Celtic Cross 134, 138, 141, 142, 145, 146, 161, 165
Romany Draw 91-92, 101, 127
success, career and 94, 103
Sun 198
Bohemian Spread 36, 40, 67, 68, 71, 72
Celtic Cross 142, 146, 153, 157, 173, 178
Romany Draw 91

Swords 201, 214,-217
Ace 214
Bohemian Spread 47, 51, 67, 71, 97
Celtic Cross 183
Romany Draw 96, 101, 123-125
Two 214
Bohemian Spread 48, 49, 54, 55
Romany Draw 120, 123
Three 215
Bohemian Spread 37, 38, 39, 41, 44, 45
Celtic Cross 172, 177
Romany Draw 92, 113
Four 215
Bohemian Spread 67, 72
Celtic Cross 171, 176
Romany Draw 86, 105-106, 110,112
Five 215
Bohemian Spread 49, 55, 59, 65
Romany Draw 121
Six 215
Bohemian Spread 37, 42, 77
Celtic Cross 163, 169
Romany Draw 90, 98, 110
Seven 216
Bohemian Spread 77
Romany Draw 91-103
Eight 216
Bohemian Spread 46, 50
Celtic Cross 162, 167
Romany Draw 88-89, 102, 125
Nine 216
Romany Draw 90-91, 103, 115, 126
Ten 216
Bohemian Spread 48, 54
Celtic Cross 161, 165, 184
Romany Draw 91, 98, 123
Knave 217
Knight 217
Bohemian Spread 69, 74
Romany Draw 105, 107, 110, 114
Queen 217
Bohemian Spread 48, 52, 69, 75, 76
Romany Draw 124
King 217
Bohemian Spread 58, 62
representing querent 16

T

Temperance 49, 55, 58, 63, 68, 73, 195
Celtic Cross 142, 143, 172, 177
Romany Draw 89, 90
Tower 196
Bohemian Spread 47, 51, 57, 61, 98
Celtic Cross 134, 138, 141, 145, 150, 151, 153-155, 158
Romany Draw 93, 100, 105

U

unexpected 77
love and 46-55

W

Wands 200, 206-209
Ace 206
Bohemian Spread 57, 61, 67, 71
Celtic Cross 163, 169
Romany Draw 102
Two 206
Bohemian Spread 59, 64

Celtic Cross 172, 176
Romany Draw 121
Three 207
Bohemian Spread 59, 65
Celtic Cross 160, 164-165
Romany Draw 101
Four 207
Bohemian Spread 37, 41, 57, 61
Romany Draw 109
Five 207
Bohemian Spread 37, 42, 58, 63
Romany Draw 124
Six 207
Bohemian Spread 66, 70-71
Celtic Cross 172, 177
Romany Draw 97, 102-103
Seven 208
Bohemian Spread 67, 72, 79
Eight 208
Bohemian Spread 77
Romany Draw 105
Nine 208
Bohemian Spread 39, 44, 59, 65, 68, 73-74
Celtic Cross 171, 175
Ten 208
Bohemian Spread 49, 55, 76
Celtic Cross 170, 174
Romany Draw 89, 100, 115
Knave 209
Romany Draw 102-103
Knight 209
Celtic Cross 184
Romany Draw 124
Queen 209
Bohemian Spread 36, 39, 40, 44
Romany Draw 92
King 209
Bohemian Spread 57, 61
Romany Draw 100
representing querent 16
well-being 104-115
Wheel of Fortune 193
Bohemian Spread 59, 64, 67, 68, 69, 71, 73, 75, 77
Celtic Cross 135, 139, 153, 158, 162, 166-167
Romany Draw 89, 105
wishes, ultimate 36-45, 77
work 79
World 119
Bohemian Spread 39, 45, 56, 60
Celtic Cross 140, 144-145, 152, 156, 162, 168
Romany Draw 101, 114